**A network of critics rave about YAP:
*The Official Young Aspiring Professional's
Fast-Track Handbook*—**

"The advice in YAP was so good, it almost made me
want to get a job!"
  —Zsa Zsa Galore, FORTUNE*hunter Magazine*

"An exploration of a new cuisine—now I know
why I crave kiwi fruit."
  —Julie Kidd, PBS *Gourmand*

"More valuable as a reference than the PDR."
  —Dr. Ben S. Pock

"In the 'Serious Interfacing' chapter, Crimmins shines
as she explains the problems of love on the fast track."
  —Ellen Girley Green, *Cosmotropolis*

"More fun than dying."
  —Elspeth Kibbler-Rice

White has been chosen as the color scheme, since its neutrality helps the eye to focus on the print and other natural accents throughout the book.

The Official
Young Aspiring Professional's
Fast-Track Handbook

C. E. Crimmins

Photography by Michael LaRiche

*Illustrations by Pamela Higgins Patrick
and Tom Barrett*

Running Press
Book Publishers
Philadelphia ◇ Pennsylvania

9   8   7   6   5   4   3   2   1
Digit on the right indicates the number of this printing.

Library of Congress Cataloging in Publication Data:
Crimmins, C.E.
    Y.A.P.: The official young aspiring professional's
fast-track handbook
    1. Professional employees—Anecdotes, facetiae,
satire, etc. I. Title. II. Title: YAP.
PN6231.P747C74 1983   818'.5402   83-16072
ISBN 0-89471-244-6 (lib. bdg.)
ISBN 0-89471-243-8 (pbk.)

William Hamilton cartoons reprinted by permission of
Chronicle Features, San Francisco. Henry Martin
cartoons reprinted by permission of Tribune Company
Syndicate, Inc. "The Neighborhood" reprinted courtesy
of Register & Tribune Syndicate, Inc. Cartoons on pages
104, 116 and back cover reprinted from the Wall Street
Journal by permission of Cartoon Features Syndicate, Inc.

Cover design by Toby Schmidt.
Cover illustration by Tom Herbert.
Typography: Text is Novarese by rci, Philadelphia, PA.
Chapter openings by Composing Room, Philadelphia, PA.
Printed by Command Web, Secaucus, NJ.

This book may be ordered by mail from the publisher. Please
include 75 cents postage. **But try your bookstore first.**

Running Press
Book Publishers
125 South 22nd Street
Philadelphia, Pennsylvania 19103

Other books inputted by C.E. Crimmins:

Press for Success: Save Millions on Dry-Cleaning Bills
  by Ironing Your Own Clothes

The Floppy Disk Workout Book: The "No Pain, No Gain" Way
  to Firm Up Your Software

Little Mary Cunningham, Happy at Last

The Totalled Woman: Gaining Sympathy Through Exhaustion

What Color is Your Parakeet? Selecting a Budgie that
  Won't Clash with the Drapes

Lower Your Profile in 30 Days: A Paranoid's Guide to Privacy

CONTENTS

I'd like to acknowledge the excellent input and feedback I received from my network: Sarah Babaian, Joellen Brown, Daniel Malone, Suzy Tiernan, Deborah McColloch, Jim Fanto, Loretta Johnson, Barbara Lancaster, Bob Urban, Nancy Veale Urban, Read Urban, Allison Scott, Judy Wicks, the Hon household (Sandy, Justin, Jay, Pam, Andy, Gwen, and Frank) and the Neighbors (St. James, Lida, Misa, and Victor), Bruce Schimmel and Chris Hill of the Philadelphia City Paper; *all my friends at Human Resources Network and Running Press; and my mentor, Mom. Last but not least, this book could not have been written without the domestic support of my connubial associate, Alan S. Forman.*

1

YAP: IT'S MORE THAN PAY SPELLED BACKWARDS.

How to tell if you are a YAP — and if not, how to become one

To Be Young, Aspiring, and Professional— The YAP Lifestyle

What is a YAP?

Remember when success wasn't something you dressed for? When people ate Sunday dinner instead of brunch? When the fast track was for express trains? Well, those days are as dead as the era of dashikis and long hair. Walk around at lunchtime in any fair-sized city in America, and chances are you'll find yourself surrounded by Young Aspiring Professionals (YAPs), who are fast becoming the emblem of the '80s. (In fact, you might even be a YAP yourself.)

Typical YAPs are 25 to 40, well-educated, well-motivated, well-dressed, and well-exercised. When you're a YAP, a young screenwriter advises, you "have other people do things for you.

You travel the city having your needs taken care of—in one place, someone fixes your hair, in another someone fixes your body, and then, at a restaurant, someone fixes you dinner." Fast-track YAPs eat out regularly, see a hair stylist at least every six weeks, make wise investments, and, with their disposable income, hire people to do things they don't have time for, due to the demands of a hectic career.

If you are a YAP-in-Transition (YAPiT), ready to take the plunge, this book will help you refine your techniques. Simply take our YQ test to find out where you stand. Then study our sure-fire strategies for moving ahead even faster and further.

7

Test your YQ (YAP Quotient) by answering these simple questions:

(1) *Have you replaced your psychotherapist with a personal financial consultant?*
   ☐ *of course*   ☐ *not yet*

Feedback: Give yourself 5 points if you answered yes, 0 if you answered negatively. If you never had a psychotherapist, but have a financial consultant anyway, give yourself 7 points. If you have both, take 6 points.

(2) *In the last year, have you employed a:*
   ☐ *dog-walker?*
   ☐ *housecleaner?*
   ☐ *caterer?*
   ☐ *plant-waterer?*
   ☐ *dating service?*
   ☐ *headhunter?*

Feedback: Add 3 points for each personal consultant checked off.

(3) *How many times did you dine out in the last two weeks?*
   A. *None to 4.*
   B. *From 4 to 7.*
   C. *Between 8 and 14.*
   D. *Won't know until my American Express bill comes in.*

Feedback: 0 points for A, 3 points for B, 7 points for C (Our compliments to the chefs!) 9 points for D.

(4) *A floppy disk is:*
   A. *part of the new computer technology.*
   B. *a back ailment requiring hospitalization.*
   C. *an old 45 RPM record left on a hot radiator.*

Feedback: 0 points for B and C (How was your three-year trip to Outer Mongolia?); 4 points for A.

(5) When you're getting ready to complete a task, you are:
   A. *finishing up.*
   B. *nearing the end.*
   C. *finalizing.*

Feedback: 0 points for A and B, 3 points for C (Very good—maximizing your use of jargon is important).

(6) *Your tax deductions last year amounted to:*
   A. *less than 30% of your salary.*
   B. *30% to 50% of your salary.*
   C. *50% to 115% of your salary.*

Feedback: 1 point for A (Get a new financial consultant); 3 points for B, 7 points for C (only if you've never been audited).

(7) IRA *stands for:*
   A. *an Individual Retirement Account.*
   B. *the Irish Republican Army.*
   C. *an Irresponsible Risk Assessment.*

Feedback: 4 points for A (Good strategic planning); 1 point for B (Accurate, but too ethnic); 6 points for C (An ability to make up meaningless acronyms can come in handy).

(8) *Do you own a(n):*
   ☐ Saab, Volvo, or BMW?
   ☐ *phone-answering machine?*
   ☐ *white cotton sofa?*
   ☐ *Cuisinart or pasta machine?*
   ☐ *espresso machine?*
   ☐ *ice cream maker?*
   ☐ Oriental *rug?*
   ☐ *wine collection?*
   ☐ *cordless telephone?*
   ☐ *paging beeper?*
   ☐ *video cassette recorder (VCR)?*
   ☐ *fish-poacher?*
   ☐ *home computer?*

Feedback: 2 points for each YAPpy accouterment you possess.

(9) *In the last 3 months, have you eaten:*
   ☐ *quiche?*
   ☐ *black bread?*
   ☐ *an avocado?*
   ☐ *a kiwi fruit?*
   ☐ *a croissant?*
   ☐ *chicken salad with green grapes?*
   ☐ *Haagen-Dazs ice cream?*
   ☐ *Brie?*

Feedback: 2 points for each delectable checked off.

(10) *Who is Eddie Haskell?*
   A. *A singer formerly with the Sex Pistols.*
   B. *Wally's friend on* Leave it to Beaver.
   C. *A manufacturer of outdoor wear.*

Feedback: 0 points for A, 6 points for B, 2 points for C (Nice try).

(11) *The last time you saw a hair stylist was:*
A. *in the last 3 weeks.*
B. *4 to 8 weeks ago.*
C. *more than 2 months ago.*

Feedback: 8 points for A, 4 points for B, 0 points for C. (Appearances are important.)

(12) Nautilus *is:*
A. *the name of the submarine in* 20,000 Leagues Under the Sea.
B. *an exercise regimen based on weight-lifting machines.*
C. *Walt Disney's new undersea singles' theme park.*

Feedback: 1 point for A (Good guess), 6 points for B, 0 points for C (Shame on you!).

(13) *Which of the following magazines, newspapers, and catalogs do you read or receive?*
A. The New Yorker *or* Vanity Fair
B. Gourmet, Bon Appétit, *or* Cuisine
C. Fortune
D. Geo
E. Money
F. *Glossy regional publication* (San Francisco, Philadelphia, Los Angeles, New York, *etc.*)
G. Scientific American
H. Metropolitan Home, Architectural Digest, *or* Holiday Homes International
I. Wall Street Journal, Boardroom Reports
J. *The Sharper Image Catalog*
K. Signature
L. Esquire
M. *Brookstone Catalog*
N. *Eddie Bauer Catalog*
O. *Local PBS monthly program guide*
P. American Express
Q. Savvy *or* Working Woman
R. *Conran's Catalog*
S. *Spencer Gifts Catalog*
T. *Radio Shack Catalog*
U. National Geographic
V. Reader's Digest
X. Popular Science *or* Hot Rod
Z. National Enquirer *or* Mercenary

Feedback: 3 points each, A–R; subtract 3 points for each for S to Z. Add 2 points for each you receive or read at the office.

ATTACK OF THE

YOUNG PROFESSIONALS!

Watch in horror as they...

...turn your neighborhood into an overpriced, high-rent boutiqueland!

...talk about their investments right in front of your eyes! Merrill Lynch says oxen, mung beans, and rare keychains!

...dress for success even while sleeping! WRONG RIGHT

Drawing by R. Chast; © 1983 The New Yorker Magazine, Inc.

(14) Networking is:
   A. a television rating system.
   B. making contacts with key people crucial to career development.
   C. a method employed by Icelandic fishermen to catch tuna.
Feedback: 0 points for A and C, 5 for B.

(15) Which television actress played a famous Pre-YAP?
   ☐ June Lockhart   ☐ Lucille Ball
   ☐ Marlo Thomas
Feedback: 0 points for June and Lucy; 6 points if you picked That Girl.

(16) You are faced with two tasks and a limited amount of time. You:
   A. decide which one is most important.
   B. get your deadlines extended.
   C. prioritize.
Feedback: 0 points for A, 3 for B, 6 for C.

(17) Your educational background is:
   A. high school graduate.
   B. college graduate.
   C. one graduate degree.
   D. two or more graduate degrees.
Feedback: 0 points for A, 3 points for B, 6 points for C, 10 points for D
(Add 6 points to any educational score if you own your own business.)

(18) How many items of clothing have you purchased on sale in the last 3 months?
   A. 0 to 2.

B. 2 *to* 5.

C. *I don't know—my wardrobe consultant doesn't tell me when something's on sale.*

Feedback: 4 points for A, 1 for B, 7 points for C. (It's good to let your consultant do the shopping.)

(19) *Do you own a house or condominium?*

A. *Yes.*

B. *No, but I am looking.*

C. *I own more than one.*

D. *No—I can't raise the down payment.*

Feedback: 6 points for A, 4 points for B, 10 points for C, 1 point for D (Never let poverty stand in the way of tax deductions!).

Scoring:

150 *and over*: Congratulations! You're no longer aspiring—you've Arrived.

100–149: Glad we could touch base like this. You're definitely on the fast track to YAPpiness.

70–99: There's hope, but you must improve your personal strategy immediately. Buy a new suit, get an expensive haircut, and eat out at least 8 times next week.

69 *and below*: There are still some marvelous opportunities for people who *want* to work on the Alaskan pipeline.

A Brief Scenario: the Birth, Education, and Evolution of YAPs

The teeming suburbs of the '50s and early '60s were the great spawning ground for YAPs. Dad looked really cute in uniform when he came back from the war, and Mom had no idea that her attraction to khaki would keep demographers and schoolteachers busy for the next 30 years. She and Dad just settled down to being fruitful and multiplying like Americans had never multiplied before. In tract households across the land, audiences for *Leave it to Beaver* and *Father Knows Best* grew by leaps and bounds. All the little population explosions added up to one big national Baby Boom.

Like most parents, Mom and Dad believed that their beloved John and Susan were gifted, intelligent, and certainly most likely to succeed. Neither parent had the slightest inkling that grown-up Boomers were going to face some tough job competition in the post-flowerchild '80s. Yet as they were to find out, their positive reinforcement of overachievement had worked subliminally on John and

Susan to prepare the little tykes for the dog-eat-dog world.

Sure, Mom and Dad had been upset in the early 1970s, when adolescents Susie and Johnny railed against their parents' "plastic" world. Johnny, who liked to smoke pot with friends and listen to Country Joe and the Fish, created his "own major" in environmental sociology at Hampshire College and worked after graduation as a VISTA volunteer. Susie left to go "cross-country" with her bearded boyfriend in a VW van. ("Thank God, she called from Boulder and we wired her the money to fly home.")

But then John suddenly decided that he wanted to go to law school. Three years after Susie moved to New York (with a B.A. in Modern Dance from Bennington), she was hired as a management trainee for Chase Manhattan Bank and began her M.B.A. at NYU's evening division.

Before they knew it, John and Susie had become YAPs.

Now they spend as much on

YAPs: Before

13

...And After

PHP

clothes each season as they once spent on a good stereo system. John arrives home from his Cleveland law firm at 9:00 each evening, pours himself a glass of Chardonnay, and heats up a Stouffer's Spinach Soufflé before sitting down to work he's brought from the office.

At 6:00 each night, Susie leaves Chase, picks up her 8-month-old daughter Jessica from her day school in a historically-certified Greenwich Village town house, takes a cab home to her apartment, and flips on her phone machine to see if there are any messages from Tom, her architect husband.

Grandma and Grandpa are happy but perplexed. Their adult children aspire toward successful careers and material goods—just as they were taught to do—yet those aspirations now take a different turn. Instead of coveting a four-bedroom house with an acre of lawn, the kids want a quaint town house with "original features." No panelled station wagon for them: a Saab or Volvo, please, and maybe (after a few years) a BMW. While their parents dreamed of having enough money to eat out once a week, John and Susan eat out more than five times a week as it is—and try to afford the time to cook *one* romantic dinner a week at home, using the Cuisinarts that gather dust on their butcherblock counters.

YAPPILY
Ever After

From Eskimo Agitator to Urban Entrepreneur: One YAP's Odyssey

Judith Wicks, 36, is co-owner of La Terrasse (one of Philadelphia's best-known French restaurants) and a successful nonprofit publisher active in such business organizations as the Mayor's Small Business Advisory Council and the Chamber of Commerce. The story of how she changed from a '60s hippie activist to an '80s entrepreneur exemplifies what being a YAP is all about.

An English major in college, Wicks became politically involved: "During the Vietnam War, my first husband and I joined VISTA because it was draft deferrable. We lived in an Eskimo village in Alaska for a year, and all the volunteers were fired for becoming politically active, helping the Eskimos understand land claims for the pipeline. We were ordered to get out of the state in 48 hours.

"We came to Philadelphia in 1970 for a friend's wedding, and liked the city so much we decided to move here from western Pennsylvania. A friend of ours who went to the University of Pennsylvania told us there were no good shops around campus. So we loaded up our Volvo station wagon with our stuff—including two dogs and a pair of doves—and headed to Philly to start a retail store."

The doves became the symbol of the couple's Free People's Store, which sold East Indian bedspreads, T-shirts, Frisbees, rolling papers, and other necessities for the college crowd. "We slept in sleeping bags on the floor of the store because we didn't have enough money to rent an apartment. We didn't have a shower, either, so we had to depend on friends' bathrooms."

The store featured a "free bin," which offered clothes *gratis* to customers and vagrants alike. Another community service the couple provided was the "Whole City Catalog," which helped neighbors find services such as draft counselling, food co-ops, minority rights agencies, and gay liberation organizations.

After Wicks and her husband split up, he went on to transform the Free People's Store into a YAP clothing and kitchenware emporium called Urban Outfitters, which now sells Izod shirts, kitchen gadgets, glassware, and cards in two Philadelphia locations, and one in Cambridge, MA. (One store recently opened in New York's Greenwich Village and another will open soon in Washington, DC.)

Wicks literally stumbled into her career as a restaurant owner when she wrecked her ex-husband's car on the way to Florida. Staring at the totalled auto, she told a passerby that she would have to get a job to pay for it. The stranger volunteered that a friend of his was quitting her job as a waitress at a French restaurant, and suggested that Wicks show up on the day his friend planned to leave. Wicks started as a part-time waitress at La Terrasse, then a small establishment near the University.

Two years later she was managing the place, and then her life "really began to change." As a waitress, she had eaten extra desserts and let her friends drink and dine for free. But once she became a manager, she had to admonish other employees against such behavior. "All of a sudden, I realized that taking pastries from the restaurant was like taking money off someone's dresser—it was stealing! And luckily, for me, society was changing while I was. People were becoming more business-oriented. There wasn't as much of a freeloader attitude.

"But it still was a difficult change for me, being the authority figure with people who were my peers, my exact own age. I'd always just worn jeans and T-shirts, so I went out and got new clothes. At the beginning, I thought I had to change my personality in order to play this role, that people working at the restaurant needed a lot of discipline and authority. After a while, I realized that a lot of people were responsible and self-disciplined, so I could more or less be myself and still be a manager. But there were a million rules that I gradually started making up and enforcing. I can still remember when I told the waiters they had to wear ties at dinner—they couldn't believe it!"

Gradually, the clientele of the restaurant changed, too. "In the early '70s, all the customers were casually dressed. We served omelets and hamburgers at dinnertime, and were definitely more geared toward professors and the student crowd. We used to all get drunk while we were working and sit on the customers' laps. Now we advertise in *The New Yorker* and *Gourmet*. At least once a month we get a limousine parked out front, with someone coming from New York or Washington just to have dinner and then drive back."

Today the restaurant grosses over $2 million a year, and Wicks still continues her community work. Her nonprofit company, Synapse, will soon publish a resource guide to child care, a subject that interests her because of her experiences as a working mother. (Wicks and her second husband, architect Neil Schlosser, have a girl, Grace, 4, and a boy, Lawrence, 2.)

The key to the kind of change she has gone through in the last ten years, Wicks believes, means getting a grasp on "the whole economic thing—understanding about money and its importance. Money is not dirty. And providing jobs for people is one of the most important things you can do for a community."

Why Anyone Can Be a YAP

Are you working in a dead-end job? Still wearing bell-bottoms? Don't even have a touch-phone, let alone a phone-answering machine? Don't despair! This book is here to help you through the evolutionary process of YAPification.

No matter that you have a degree in East European folklore or a résumé that lists stints as a lifeguard, short-order cook, and social worker. YAPs naturally evolve via what is known as "a well-planned career strategy." (Translation: "How in the world am I going to make some money?")

The Enviable Résumé: Reading Between the Lines

The roads to becoming a successful YAP are many, as countless personal stories attest. But for getting on the fast track to fame and fortune, there are really only three career strategies that cannot fail:

(1) The Professional Degree

Under this plan (called the "initial strategy," and not because it comes first), anyone (even a teacher of macramé) can redeem him- or herself. Simply postpone "real life" for a number of years by returning to school, and affix those all-important initials (M.B.A., J.D., M.D.) to your last name.

Drawbacks: The cost of a good initial-accruing program is formidable. Three years of Ivy League law school, for example, can set you back up to $30,000 in tuition alone. Plus you *do* have to study, which can get to be a drag when you're over 25.

Advantages: Mom and Dad will probably be relieved that you're trading in your five-year dream of constructing an electric harpsichord in favor of a Harvard M.B.A., and so are likely to be an easy touch for tuition expenses. Though studying is pretty boring, it beats working, and you can wear all your jeans and T-shirts from your college days—if they still fit you. Upon graduation, moreover, you will be an instant YAP—no muss, no fuss, no taking an "entry-level" position. You'll never have to sit in front of a typewriter again.

(2) The Entrepreneurial Route

Would-be YAPs who want to adopt this strategy should carefully study the market, put on their thinking chapeaux, and figure out what indispensable product, fad, or service is waiting to take America by storm. In your strategizing, do not be afraid to break with age-old traditions. Remember, for example, that before Snuglis (the cloth baby pouch), parents actually *carried* infants with their own two hands.

Drawbacks: It's sometimes hard to raise capital for ventures that less creative minds term "frivolous." Sure, you know your Chablis-flavored toothpaste is the biggest thing to hit since the Pet Rock. But Mom and Dad would really rather see you use your chemistry degree to go back to medical school instead of perfecting a product that will give winos the whitest teeth in town.

Advantages: The money you make is all yours, and you get a lot of media attention. The savvy entrepreneur is a familiar YAP type, and journalists like to write human-interest stories about high school dropouts who make a fortune marketing liver paté ice cream franchises. Why, Snugglies were even written up in the *Wall Street Journal*!

(3) The Clawing-Your-Way-to-the-Top Approach

The least YAPpy of the three, not recommended for the faint of heart. Starting in a lower-level job out of college (an undergraduate degree *is* a must), you resolve to fast-track it into the inner circle of upper management by your late twenties or early thirties. It's a dirty career, but someone has to do it.

Disadvantages: Before your natural abilities can be recognized and rewarded, you will have to suffer the slings and arrows of outrageous mediocrity. It will be a constant struggle to set yourself apart from the other plebians.

Advantages: During your climb to the top, you're earning a salary and networking along the way. You'll learn a lot about job titles. Most probably you will be given free business cards, which you can hand out in singles bars. And, if you *do* experience a meteoric rise in career stature, you can exaggerate the very brief time you spent in the trenches to enhance your credibility. ("Hell, when I started, we worked eleven hours a day.")

Places You Can Find YAPs: Bars decorated with potted ferns, furniture stores that sell butcher block tables, elevators of high-rise office buildings, country inns, personal computer stores, stress management clinics.

Places where YAPs Will Not Be Caught Dead: bowling alleys, McDonald's; Sears, Roebuck & Co. stores; Howard Johnson's, bus terminals, free clinics, and unemployment offices.

Things that Embarrass YAPs: Bar Mitzvah pictures, First Communion photos, laminated diplomas, pictures of self and siblings at the Land of Make Believe or Santa's Workshop, being discovered as the owner of a copy of a Clint Eastwood movie.

A Field Guide
to Fast-Trackers

YAPs come in all shapes and colors, genders and sizes. A lot of people were born during those Baby Boom years and if you expect to build a useful network of contacts, you must learn to recognize your fellow YAPs in all their manifestations. At any wine-tasting party or Peter, Paul and Mary concert, you're likely to run into a number of the following types:

SuperYAP

Recognized by the dark circles under his eyes. (He sleeps only three hours a night, believing that quality time is the only thing that counts, even when it comes to shut-eye.) Lines between this guy's worklife and home-life have blurred to the point that he no longer knows if he is making friends or networking, deciding on something or prioritizing, asking someone's opinion or requesting feedback.

Tends to answer his home phone "John Jones." Waits for the beep, even after he's reached a real person. Were it possible, he'd install an answering machine on the radio phone in his BMW.

Hard-Edged, Dressed-for-Success Female YAP

If this woman has come to YAPdom a mite late, she will make up for lost time. She usually comes with two sets of papers: an M.B.A. from a prestigious institution, and a divorce decree from a foolish first marriage to a slow-track buffoon. *Attire:* Basic business suit with A-line skirt, shirt with silk tie, and tasteful black pumps. Wears her hair pulled back or cut in a severe style. A serious worker who rarely smiles or laughs. Tries to avoid having sex with people in her office building because "you never know if it'll get around."

Mr. Junior Executive

Knew he wanted to be a financial advisor since the age of three. Started reading the *Wall Street Journal* while still in junior high. Junior Achievement. Bought his first stock at 15. Won Kiwanis scholarship for civic service upon graduating from high school. At 17, got a part-time job so he could buy a Honda. As a Wharton undergraduate, started a cleaning service for student apartments. Watches *Wall Street Week* and not *Hill Street Blues.*

Other YAPs distrust him because of his lack of ambivalence about the fast-track life. Since he's never done anything unrelated to business, Mr. Junior Executive doesn't quite fit in, especially at parties, where he requests feedback on a new format for his firm's annual report. After one or two glasses of Chablis, most YAPs want to talk about that former, more meaningful time in their lives when they were poets or musicians.*

Such memories are usually grossly exaggerated—the former occupations merely represent undergraduate majors.

Sexy Female YAP

Popular in business circles because she flirts well and likes to swear—which, in an attractive woman, drives men wild. She reads *Playboy* and is apt to let that drop at parties. More frequently involved in business side of a creative profession—publishing, advertising, music, food—than in some strictly business enterprise like banking. *Attire:* Split skirt, unbuttoned blouse, high heels, and open-toed shoes. Suit coat seems specially cut to strain at her breasts when buttoned. Curly hair, blunt-cut or permed. Her idea of "dressing for success" just might be a Danskin leotard underneath a blazer.

When dating, since she's not secure about her role or her intelligence, she is most likely to feel comfortable with non-YAP men. She may enjoy going out with truck drivers—but not to anywhere her co-workers would see her.

Nerd YAP

The guy who struck it rich and successful with an idea earning millions of dollars. Nobody knows how he made so much money. He was a nerd and always will be, but people now think of him as on the fast track to success. No longer "aspiring" for money, but for some semblance of normalcy. A real loner.

Computer types are the prime example of this YAP category. (We call this type of success the Steven Jobs syndrome.) Nerd YAPs make great human-interest stories in *People* magazine, and generally enjoy lots of attention from gold-digger YAP females.

Bohemian or Counter-Culture YAP

Attire: Handcrafted, coordinated costume that costs hundreds of dollars. Gives parties that bring together all sorts of YAPs, and sometimes even introduces *real* bohemians—long-haired artists who spit on the floor—to her YAP clients/friends. Either never got over the comforts of '60s dressing, or fancies herself "artistic." Might be married to a doctor or lawyer, and runs her own restaurant, gourmet cooking shop, clothing store, or art gallery. At the very least, married to a college professor considering a second career (See "Late-Blooming YAP"). If she has children, they are named Jason and Sara. Hasn't cut her hair, or wishes she hadn't because of all those beautiful handcrafted combs from Spain.

The Gay Male YAP

Responsible for YAPpifying more urban town houses than all the other types put together. *Attire:* Tastefully subdued Italian suit, expensive watch, silk tie with geometric design. Violates business' unspoken dictum against wearing jewelry by sporting an expensive ring on one or both hands.

Sometimes comes as half of a couple, who work as interior decorators, art directors, bankers, accountants, restaurateurs, etc. Lots of disposable income (never having to worry about orthodontist bills, private school tuition, or alimony payments).

The Minority YAP

Works in the Public Sector dispensing government funds. Bright, alienated; when speaking, uses perfect diction but peppers conversation with minority slang to emphasize his roots. Dresses more formally than others at his job level, but still owns one dashiki for at-home wear. Goes out with WASPs.

Lives in a town house apartment decorated with African artifacts; bookshelves filled with the works of Richard Wright, James Baldwin, W.E.B. DuBois, and the Harlem Renaissance poets. Extensive jazz collection.

The YAP's YAP

Serves other YAPs as bartender, waiter, caterer, or hair stylist. Successful because most career types want to unwind with people at their own educational level—after all, who wants a waitress who can't discuss Christo, Proust, Buckminster Fuller, or Jasper Johns?

The typical YAP bartender has at least a master's degree, if not a Ph.D., in some area of the humanities, and makes about $40,000 a year (and he doesn't even have to wear a suit every day!).

Politically-Liberal YAP

Sometimes hard to single out unless he or she has gone public enough to wear a campaign button or a "Save the Whales" tie. Works for Exxon during the day and then "gets down" with the people at political rallies at night. Possesses tremendous powers of rationalization, believing that it's better for someone like him—a sort of watchdog on corporate America—to hold down his position, rather than for a real bastard with no social conscience.

To accommodate this liberal type, corporations have created entire departments—watch for him in Public Affairs, Community Relations, and Human Resources.

Late-Blooming YAP

Pushing the limits of YAPdom because he's nearing 40 or a bit over. *Attire:* Tweed coat, showing a connection to academia or the bohemian life. Usually a college professor or former wanderer who got a good idea for a second career. ("Good ideas" include restaurants, consulting firms, herbal tea companies, and screenplays.) Decided to become a YAP because he never seemed to make enough money for a good vacation.

Wife into natural foods. Son broke his heart when he decided (as a freshman) to major in accounting.

2

WORKING

■ YAP CAREER MOTTO:

VENI, VIDI, PRIORIFICAVI
(I came, I saw, I prioritized)

"W-or-k?"
—Maynard G. Krebs
(Famous Non-YAP), circa 1963

Despite humongous gobs of disposable income, being a YAP isn't all fun and games and mad shopping sprees at personal computer stores. The essential ingredient of YAP life is *work*. And remember, YAPs don't hold jobs, they enjoy *careers*. Frenetic travel, overtime hours (without pay, of course, since you are *professional*), and a constant search for contacts go with the territory.

All YAPs love their careers. Even if you'd rather be home watching *Donahue*, act publicly as if your entire emotional life revolves around what you do for a living. If you expect anyone to take you seriously, you must speak about the earning experience constantly. When discussing your career at parties or at office lunches, use words like "challenging," "fulfilling," and "mind-stretching." Do not be afraid to appear driven—in a recent ad campaign, Fortune Magazine told us that it's all right to be ambitious again.

But this dedication to work needn't hamper your personal style. Feel free to communicate your intense love of career according to your personality and the job you've chosen. For example:

•*The laid-back, confident approach:* "Yes, things went pretty well for us last year . . . We've got a couple of interesting things going on . . . I just made a move that I think will be very good for me, *and* the company. . . ."

•*The tight-lipped, mysterious approach*: "Yes, my work is very demanding . . . No, I'm not in the high technology field, exactly . . . I'd love to, but something big is just breaking. . . ."

•*The overtime, angst-ridden approach*: "I don't know why I still love this job, but I do . . . Do you know I worked eighty-three hours last week? . . . If I don't do it, who will?"

Salaries: The $25,000 Initiation Fee

You're really only a YAP-in-Transition (YAPiT) if you make substantially less than $25,000 a year. Even 25 g's—standard entry-level earnings for a YAP—leave you with a paltry amount of discretionary spending power. To a SuperYAP, $25,000 is the amount he made on his first stock market killing.

If you aren't yet bringing in $25,000, the name of the game is

Every YAP needs a pocketful of plastic.

pretense. To help you look like you're earning even more, here are some tips:

•U*se many credit cards*. For first impressions, you'll want to have an American Express. Although it's definitely the status card to own, unfortunately Amex expects you to pay for your purchases in full

when you receive the bill. We also suggest getting at least six other cards—including Visa, Master-Card, and assorted department-store accounts—to space out your credit purchases and stretch your nearly non-existent salary a bit further.

•*Give substantial amounts of money to Public Television*. Anyone who's endured the "pledge nights" knows by heart the premiums offered for contributing money to the local PBS station. Give enough to earn a really neat gift. (You can charge it, and the money's tax-deductible.) Then, when your friends see Richie Havens' picture of a whale framed on your wall, they'll assume that you directed some of your disposable income to a worthy cause.

•*Invest in an expensive watch or briefcase.* More than anything else, these two items tell the world how much money you're able to toss off for seemingly utilitarian objects. (For both items, the thinner the better.) Choose a timepiece or business satchel that puts you just at your credit limit on one of your cards.

A note on dual earning power: Although Mom and Dad say that

In Search of Tax Deductions.

Almost as much fun as making money is plotting how to keep the IRS from taking it away from you. A whole new world opens up for the fledgling earner who discovers the Zen of the creative tax return.

Fun deductions for you to try:

Expense	Deduct as
Magazine subscriptions	Educational expenses
Paying kid to rake leaves	Real estate maintenance
Case of Johnny Walker	Stress management seminar
Doggie dental bills	Health expenditures
Purchase of VCR and Atari video games	Home office expenses
Gift to lover at work	Business-related expense
Magnum of Dom Perignon, consumed over candlelit dinner	Uninsured loss

Tax deductions that don't work: depreciation of your Monkees albums, business clothing expenses.

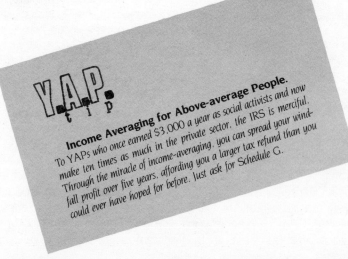

Y.A.P. tip

Income Averaging for Above-average People.

To YAPs who once earned $3,000 a year as social activists and now make ten times as much in the private sector, the IRS is merciful. Through the miracle of income-averaging, you can spread your windfall profit over five years, affording you a larger tax refund than you could ever have hoped for before. Just ask for Schedule G.

"two can live cheaper than one," don't believe it. Remember, you're paying for two phone-answering machines and two sets of dry-cleaning bills. Respectable YAP couples should be pulling in at least $50,000 between them.

Your Investment Scoresheet

Boring but necessary places to keep some money: Individual Retirement Accounts, money market funds, savings certificates.

Non-YAP financial arrangements: U.S. Savings Bonds, Christmas and Vacation Clubs, passbook savings accounts, state lottery, off-track betting.

Responsible things to invest in: Oriental rugs, raku pottery, antique furniture, real estate, Krugerrands (unless you are politically liberal), stocks and bonds, venture capital operations, Mercedes.

Non-YAP investments: Elvis Presley memorabilia, Olympic gold coins, Franklin Mint miniatures, Wedgwood Christmas plates, Hallmark holiday ornaments, McGovern/Eagleton buttons, Bicentennial coffins.

Photo Quiz: YAP and Non-YAP collectibles. Find the item[s] that any YAP would be proud to display.

Answer: If you chose (B), you accurately spotted the lone YAP *objet d'art* in this otherwise unrelieved collection of tackiness. It's a handmade raku bowl. (H) is a nice guess, since it's the flag of the Smithsonian Institution, but no true YAP would cherish such a souvenir.

Bank Machines: A YAP's Best Friend

Because you don't keep banker's hours, you need an electromagnetic bank machine card to let you make deposits and withdrawals at night and on weekends. Play this card right, and you'll never have to stand in line again—or have to deal with a live teller. (Let's face it, they dress kind of tacky, anyway, and sometimes give you less-than-crisp bills.) When dealing with your automatic teller, remember the following rules:

•Does your bank let you program a greeting to yourself for the beginning of each transaction? *Never* choose words that will embarrass you when people read them over your shoulder. ("HI, SCHMUCK," and "HERE AGAIN?" are two electronic greetings to avoid.)

•If you have more than one bank machine card, check to make sure you have the right slab of plastic for the right machine. One YAP we know shut down a whole terminal by trying to use one bank's card in another's automatic teller. (And fellow YAPs can get violent if they realize someone among them has sabotaged their plans for instant cash.)

•Never keep your bank cards next to one another—or next to credit cards with electromagnetic strips. Close contact can cause cards to "de-magnetize," rendering them useless. If you are unlucky enough to have this happen, it will *always* occur at midnight when you're on your way to that cute little cappucino-and-pastry shop around the corner that doesn't take American Express.

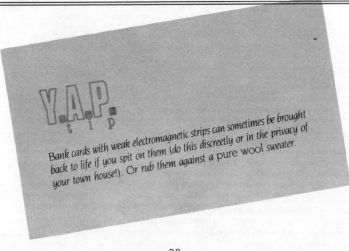

Y.A.P. tip

Bank cards with weak electromagnetic strips can sometimes be brought back to life if you spit on them (do this discreetly or in the privacy of your town house!). Or rub them against a pure wool sweater.

A Crush of Consultants

All YAPs want to be consultants—those freelance gurus of the white-collar work scene. Two career paths lead to lucrative consulting practices. Either you work for a large company, steal all their secrets, and set off on your own (the "Son of Silicon Valley" strategy). Or else you figure out how to re-package information that everybody already knows. (One YAP consulting firm obtains government information freely available to any citizen, then sells it to *Fortune* 500 companies for a hefty fee.)

Planning to set up your own consulting business? Here's a guide to help you choose an appropriate field.

Area of consultation	What it really entails
Strategic Planning	Extrapolating possible trends from information gleaned from newspaper fillers.
Corporate Social Responsibility	Telling companies how much they have to contribute to the United Way before minority groups stop complaining. Also, producing pamphlets like "Why You're Special: The DES Daughter."
Human Resources	Helping firms hire and fire whomever they want, without getting sued.
Marketing	Giving presentations about Hispanic children's growing awareness of Cocoa Puffs.
Personal Lifestyle	Hiring people to clean busy people's apartments. (See "The YAP's Time-Saving Support Network.")
Compensation	Deciding how little to pay people.
Labor Relations	Union-busting.
Image	Advising executives on what color socks to wear.
External and Internal Communications	Helping executives learn to read, write, and speak.
Community Relations	Supervising plant closings in the dead of night.
International Relations	Targeting countries with cheap labor forces.
Government Affairs	Lobbying against irresponsible radicals who want to regulate the corporate cornerstones of America's free-enterprise system.
Quality of Worklife	Hanging brightly-colored prints on office walls.

Get rid of that boring occupational title, and watch the bucks come rolling in!
To become part of the lucrative consulting biz, there's no need to go into a special corporate field. Just look closely at what you're doing now. Even if your profession is low on the YAP scale (or not even there), a little imagination will enable you to charge $100 an hour or more for your services.

Old job description	Consulting title
writer	Developmental Prose Consultant
teacher	Educational Information Consultant
salesperson	Consultant, persuasive psychology and monetary exchange
short-order cook	Consultant, strategically-planned food intake
housewife	Consultant, domestic affairs, specializing in internal communication and transportation needs
dog walker	Ambulatory Canine Consultant

YAP Professions

Low on the YAP status scale: fast-food restaurant manager, scientist, graduate student in the humanities, ultrasound technician, child-care worker.

Respectable YAP professions: city planner, architect, doctor, accountant, lawyer, restaurant owner, stockbroker, banker.

The top YAP careers: entrepreneur, financial analyst, stress management counselor, senior vice president (of almost anything), consultant of any stripe.

Non-YAP Professions too low to rate on the scale: plumber, undertaker, washroom attendant, clerk, janitor, toll-taker, garbage collector, puppeteer, dolphin trainer, forest ranger, movie usher, potter, artist, housewife, wet nurse, gardener, housekeeper.

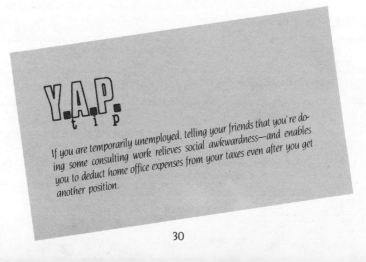

Y.A.P. tip

If you are temporarily unemployed, telling your friends that you're doing some consulting work relieves social awkwardness—and enables you to deduct home office expenses from your taxes even after you get another position.

YAPspeak: a Glossary

Practice using these terms and phrases while maintaining good eye contact and a straight face.

burnout (*n.*)—state of depression and spiritual paralysis induced by stressful working conditions and/or too much cappuccino and cocaine.

critical mass (*n.*)—level of importance; used with issues or situations. As in, "That problem is reaching critical mass."

cutting-edge (*adj.*)—slightly before its time; avant-garde. As in, "This is really cutting-edge (*Gee, I never heard of that before*)."

down side (*n.*)—disadvantages; used with *on*. As in, "On the down side, we have the enormous cost of energy to keep the plant open."

D.Y.P.O.G. (*n.*)—Dynamic Young Person On the Go. Derisive label for anyone who has just gotten a promotion over you.

fast track 1. (*n.*)—the achievement path of least resistance, the way to the top often used with *on*. As in "on the fast track". 2. (*adj.*) ambitious, successful. 3. (*v.*) to rise to the top quickly. Often used in participial form with *it*; "He's fast-tracking it (*Wow, is he stepping on a lot of backs to get ahead*)."

feedback (*n.*)—another person's opinion or advice. As in, "I'm waiting for feedback (*That idiot can't make up his mind*)."

finalize (*v.*)—to finish a task. As in, "Let me finalize my eyes (*Let me finish putting on my eye makeup*)."

gentrify (*v.*)—to make a neighborhood fit for young professionals; to drive out undesirables with rubber tire planters.

get back (*v.*)—to return someone's call. As in, "Let me get back to you (*You'll be lucky if I call you next year*)."

impact (*v.*)—influence, affect (formerly used only in reference to wisdom teeth). As in, "How will this impact our operations? (*What the hell's going to happen now?*)"

input 1. (*n.*)—suggestions made by people, or information typed into a machine. Used frequently in same sentence with *feedback*. 2. (*v.*) to write on a word processor or type information into a computer. As in, "I'll input that memo this afternoon."

interface (*v.*)—to communicate with another person or computer (not to be confused with the material inside shirt collars).

leverage (*v.*)—to get the greatest results possible from available financial or political resources.

lunch (*n.*)—midday meal or important business transaction. As in, "Let's have lunch."

network 1. (v.)—to meet people with similar interests and ambitions who might be able to help you later on. 2. (n.) a group of people who support your career and personal actions.

pencil in (v.)—to write in a luncheon or dinner date in pocket calendar. As in, "I'm pencilling you in (*We're on unless something better comes along*)."

prioritize (v.)—to decide what to do first. As in, "John, prioritize your options and let me know your decision (*Make up your own mind!*)."

push buttons and pull levers (v.)—to manipulate people or events to achieve desired results. As in, "We need to push all the right buttons and pull all the right levers."

renaissance (adj.)—renovated, revitalized, or rehabilitated. Used to describe area of city On the Way Up; as in, "located in the renaissance section."

scenario (n.)—a vivid description of what might happen next.

state-of-the-art (adj.)—at the peak of its form; as in, "Dessert was a state-of-the-art cheesecake."

strategize (v.)—to make plans or wild guesses.

touch base (v.)—to communicate briefly with another person. As in, "Let's touch base on that (*Can't you see I'm too busy to talk now?*)."

up side (n.)—a positive point. Used with *on* (See "down side").

what you're saying (n.)—a second party's opinion. As in, "I hear what you're saying, but . . .''

"Why don't my parents understand?"
A YAP's Search for Contentment
A New York lawyer in his early thirties, feeling that his career was not fulfilling, told his parents he wanted to find another job he could truly love. His perplexed parents replied, "Listen, you *love* a woman, you *like* your job."

Networking: How to get to know a whole bunch of people you don't really like, but who can help you later on.

As real YAPs understand, the workplace is not a meritocracy. If you expect to get ahead, it isn't enough to labor hard and look good—you've got to know some people in high places to give you a hand up the corporate ladder.

You never know who might make it to the top first, so it's good to start cultivating early acquaintanceships with colleagues in your field and in related industries. "Networking" through business cards is as popular as collecting baseball cards and autographs was in fifth grade, and actually the idea is very similar. Even if you don't like the person you just met, you'll want his or her business card for future reference. Like autographs, you won't even look at 75% of the cards you collect. (How many kids' signatures below "Yours 'til Niagara Falls" do you still recognize in your old yearbook?) But when you choose to hit

Actual "Guidelines for Successful Networking" at Networking "Assemblages"

(as annotated by the Nervous Networker)

[handwritten: est you forget:]

1. Always wear a visible identifying tag with your name and what you do. *[handwritten: — People like to fold them & use]*

2. Don't forget to bring extra business cards to *[handwritten: them to steady]* exchange at Assemblages. *[handwritten: wobbly restaurant tables.]*

3 . Circulate, introduce yourself, and start conversations with people you do not know. When a new person approaches, be friendly and assertive by making introductions. *[handwritten: —Especially if you haven't followed rule #1.]*

4. Specifically ask people what their business or profession is. This is an ideal time to exchange business cards. *[handwritten: — Unless you forget to bring extras.]*

[handwritten: Always bring extra rope to assemblages.]

5. Do *not* stay with the people who came with you; however, when meeting someone you already know, tie into the networking he or she is doing.

6. Have a clear idea of your goals, and anticipate unexpected opportunities in order to make the most of them. *[handwritten: —If opportunities are truly unexpected, how can you anticipate them?]*

7. Center the majority of your discussion on ways of mutually supporting one another's plans, deals, productivity, etc. This tack helps avoid too much small talk. *[handwritten: Stare at the ceiling & start singing the theme song]*

[handwritten: Put stickers on their backs so you don't count them twice.]

8. Discipline yourself to politely end repetitious *[handwritten: from "Gilligan's]* conversations. When discussions start to drag, end them! *[handwritten: Island."]*

9. Try to network with a minimum of 15 to 25 people at each Assemblage.

10. When you sense a mutual understanding with *[handwritten: (or person)]* someone during a conversation, grab that moment to make an after-business-hours or lunch appointment for further discussion.

11. Set a goal each time to make at least two future business dates. *[handwritten: —Forge ahead & put your own neck on the line.]*

12. Never wait for others to say how they can help you.

13. Remember: Whom you know is definitely as important as what you know. Simple observation of methods used by successful people should prove this to you. Assemblages are for "meeting people who could change your entire life."

the Career Path again, it's that other 25% that can make all the difference.

Here's how networking works: You hear from a former college roommate that his chemistry teaching assistant's ex-wife's corporation might have an opening in its Public Affairs department.

You call your friend's instructor's ex-wife and ask her out to lunch. She's living with the head of the Human Resources department, who promises that he will get back to you with information about the job. But while you're waiting around for his call, you remember that you met a woman at a bar six months ago who is an administrative assistant in the company's Community Relations group. You still have her business card, so you call to say that you're just touching base—and then casually ask her to dinner.

By the time the Human Re-

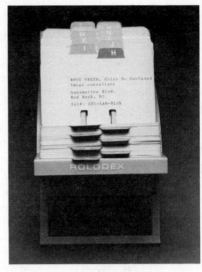

Essential networking equipment

sources director calls back to say that he's set up an interview, you have a superb grasp of the company's plans for the next few years, and could even draw a personnel flow chart if need be.

The YAP's Safety Net

*Oh, what a tangled web we weave
when first we practice to achieve.
(—with apologies to Samuel Pepys)*

Not all networking takes place with the pseudo-formal exchange of business cards. Imagine that you are forced to look for another job. Now, take inventory of your personal relationships. How many crucial connections could mean the difference between easing your way into the career of your dreams and driving a cab?

If you can think of one person each of these people knows who could have lunch with you to discuss job opportunities, then your personal network has no holes in it. If you're at a loss to identify these folks' contacts, don't go walking any tightropes.

Keep a Networking Notebook in which you place programs, business cards, and other relevant pieces of paper from events you've attended. One YAP we know takes notes about conversations she had with people at parties and receptions.

The Stress of Success: A Self-Scoring Quiz

A true YAP is a stressed YAP. Unless part of your waking day is devoted to controlling, managing, and talking about your stress, you just might not be on the fast track. To determine how much stress you're under, take the following quiz:

1. You are caught in a traffic jam, and realize that you will be at least 30 minutes late for work. Do you:
   A. Turn on the car radio, listen to classical music, and dictate a memo into your microcassette recorder?
   B. Start swearing under your breath and blow the horn?
   C. Jump from the car, open the trunk and get a crowbar, smash the windows of three cars around you, and begin chanting, "Free Lanes for Free People"?

(Answers: A: Good way to handle stress. B: Need to work on it. C: Favorite TV show is *The Incredible Hulk.)*

2. In the past 12 months, have you
- been employed?
- been unemployed?
- moved?
- not moved?
- been pregnant?
- not been pregnant?
- been divorced?
- been married?
- been single?

(Scoring: A "yes" answer to *any* of the above indicates an extreme level of stress.)

Switching Lanes on the Fast Track

Chances are your dad stayed with the same company for years, if not for a lifetime. But why let a little thing like loyalty stand in the way of better stock options? Monogamous career patterns have gone the way of monogamous relationships, and it's now acceptable to leave a position after six months' service if offered a glossier job title.

In fact, a certain amount of job-hopping helps convince future employers that you're a person in demand. If you've been with the same company for more than two years (especially without significant promotion), the romance has probably gone out of your job. Your employer could be taking you for granted. But be prepared for Mom and Dad's shocked reaction to your promiscuous career hops. They'll want to know how you can accumulate more than three W-2 forms a year and still respect yourself in the morning.

From Yippy to YAP: Jerry Rubin's Networking Salon

Every Wednesday night at 5:00 P.M., over a thousand young businesspersons arrive at Manhattan's Studio 54 to attend Jerry Rubin's Networking Salon. Rubin, once leader of the radical Yippies during the late '60s, charges YAPs $8 a session to talk over a background of soft classical music.

Each attending YAP leaves a business card with the doorman; later, Rubin sorts the guests' cards into four piles, in descending order of importance. People in the "A" and "B" piles—presidents of corporations or YAPs with other important positions—get to co-host future networking soirées and invite their own guests.

Rubin has plans to franchise his business networking salons to 36 other American cities: "I really haven't changed all that much. It's the generation that has changed. Now people are into business and success and accomplishment. But I'm still trying to bring people together. Someone has said that what I'm actually doing is sponsoring business be-ins."

Stress-Related YAP Diseases

Your credibility as a workaholic is enhanced should you suffer from any of the following stress-related disorders:

• *TMJ (Temporo-Mandibular Joint) Syndrome.* Victims of this executive's malady clench and grind their teeth under stress, tightening and cramping the muscle joint around the jaw. One YAP periodontist prescribes "support therapy" for the pain TMJ syndrome causes and runs a consulting service for corporations with afflicted executives.

• *Adult Acne.* Dermatologists see a surge in pimples caused not by chocolate milkshakes, but by escalating career demands. YAP females are particularly vulnerable to these post-pubescent break-outs.

• *Burnout.* The ultimate YAP disease. Victims' brains and personalities short-circuit due to over-stimulation and excessive demands on their time. This affliction can get you a nice, long rest away from the office. (See "The Joy of Burnout," below.)

The Joy of Burnout
(How to Fake it and Get Sympathy)

How burned do you have to be before you're *really* burned out? One way to avoid *total* burnout is to fake it about six months before actually reaching the end of your fuse. Let's face it, you need a rest. Try one or more of the following tactics and earn yourself the emotional support of co-workers—and maybe a long weekend at your boss' country place.

•Start wearing your Nikes with your suit even at the office. Or better yet, wear your jogging suit with business pumps.

•Begin reciting poetry around the office. A favorite with pre-burnout sufferers:

> My candle burns
>   at both its ends,
> It will not last the night,
> But oh my foes,
>   and ah, my friends,
> It gives a lovely light.

(—Edna St. Vincent Millay) Another favorite on the theme of burning (if you have a lot of time):

Commuter YAPs waiting impatiently to ride the rails

"The Cremation of Sam McGee" by Robert W. Service.

•Shave your head, but leave some stubble in the shape of the company logo.

Second (and Post-Burnout) Careers

Almost every YAP has plans and dreams for a second, slower-track career to which he or she can switch after burnout or after the first million dollars, whichever comes first.

Acceptable Second Careers: Vintner, sailboat charter captain, owner of Bed and Breakfast inn, homesteader, gardener, antique shop owner, caterer, artist, writer, clown, Congressional lobbyist.

Unacceptable Second Careers: Blood donor, stripper, politician, gravedigger; Tupperware, Amway, or Mary Kay cosmetics salesperson; evangelist.

YAP WRAPS

Clothing and Accessories for the Fast Track

Dressing for executive success is now old hat (or should we say old suit?). Not all YAPs adhere to John Molloy's rigid guidelines for successfully drab dressing (especially not Bohemians, Sexy Females, and Late-Bloomers). But all worry secretly about the impression their clothing makes. It's also fashionable to marvel at what you used to get away with, back before you began your career climb. "I can't believe it," says a successful restaurateur, once a waitress. "In the middle of the winter, I used to wear a black leotard and tights, cut-off denim shorts, boots, and a thick leather belt."

What some YAPs (but never Mr. Junior Executive) used to wear to conduct daily business in "the old days": T-shirts, Levi's, overalls, leotards, cut-offs, flannel shirts, engineer caps, long underwear shirts, bandanas (on head), East Indian sundresses.

> "*Wardrobe engineering, like all sciences, is really amoral. In our money-oriented, status-conscious society, most people want to succeed. And you stand a much better chance of succeeding if you know what research has determined to be the look of success.*"
> (—John Molloy, The Woman's Dress for Success Book)

Investing in Yourself:
Clothes Make the YAP

Advertisements pushing a business wardrobe make it sound as if buying a pinstriped suit is the first move toward establishing a trust fund for your children. "It makes excellent economic sense to invest in yourself," reads one women's clothing store brochure. "The yield could be higher than you could ever imagine."

Like many busy YAPs, you may be more than happy to invest in yourself, but just don't have the free moments to peruse the stores and put together outfits that bespeak power and authority (much less ones that are simply color-coordinated). But now there are professionals who can help you dress for success. They're called personal shopping consultants, image consultants, or wardrobe engineers.

In 1980, there were 40 such image consulting firms in the country; 1982 saw the number grow to 71. One New York consultant credits the increase to a competitive job market. "Everyone has a degree and credentials. They want that extra something a professional image consultant offers."

Just how does an image consultant help keep you on the fast track? In pricey personal sessions and small seminars, these wardrobe experts let you in on the suit's statistically-proven success rate. One consulting company boasts that its clients learn how to "make or break" a business suit with accessories. Better dressing habits, say these consultants, "could change your career and your life."

Don't even have the time to attend a session? Wardrobe consultants can go even one step further. For a not-so-small fee ($200 and

GREY MATTERS

up), they will shop for you and deliver new duds to your home or office. Says a harried Cleveland career woman, "In two or three hours, a shopping consultant can get me completely organized. I just tell her I need four outfits for work and two dinner dresses, and she calls me when they're ready. It's the easiest thing in the world."

The Consultant of a Different Color

You might want to go beyond mere wardrobe-consulting to a more comprehensive approach. Color consultants believe that each person's appearance is enhanced by a certain set of colors characteristic of one of the four seasons. At the end of a session of draping colorful swatches around your face and oohing and aahing, they say, "Why, you're definitely a winter person. I'm surprised you would even consider wearing burnt orange."

The color consultant will then offer to redesign your wardrobe to include your best color schemes. Joanne Nicholson of California's Color 1, whose clients include the Beach Boys (summer people?), insists that "color consultation simplifies your life . . . everything you own goes with everything else, and it helps avoid costly mistakes."

One young designer is an enthusiastic convert to color consulting. Having learned that she's an autumn person "opened up a whole new avenue that I never thought of before." Trying to discover your color spectrum on your own, she says religiously, is for "people who are just reaching out in the dark."

Finding your proper set of colors might be the '80s version of finding your mantra. But one caveat: some YAPs who have visited more than one color consultant have come away finding out that they are men and women for all seasons. Of course, if success hasn't knocked at your door since you started wearing autumn colors, you can always go to another consultant to be fitted with a spring-shaded wardrobe. But to avoid such multi-seasonal confusion, we advise the following:

1. Never go to more than one consultant — what you don't know can't hurt you.
2. If you do go to two consultants and one tells you you're a winter and the other a summer, move to Florida where there aren't any temptations to be a seasonal cross-dresser.
3. Buy a wardrobe for each set of colors. Then hire a full-time telephone adviser to tell you what seasonal vibrations the tone of your voice exudes on a particular day.
4. Throw out your record of Vivaldi's *Four Seasons*.
5. Dress only in gray jumpsuits.

The Nationwide Network of YAP Color Consultants

Color 1 Associates (*Washington and California*) 290 consultants in 50 states, serving about 40,000 new clients a year. Costs about $75 for one- to two-hour private consultation.

Color Me Beautiful (*Virginia*) 160 consultants in 38 states and around the world including Panama and Japan, serving about 5,900 clients monthly. Company headquarters in McLean, VA, Seattle, and Dallas. Costs $55 for a two-and-a-half hour class or $75 for an all-day workshop.

Beauty for All Seasons—Founded in Idaho Falls, Idaho. More than 5,000 consultants in the U.S. and Canada. Costs $35 to $150 per consultation.

The YAP's Guide to Stores with Personal Shopping Consultants

Bergdorf Goodman (*New York*)
Bonwit Teller (*Boston, Chicago, New York*)
Dayton's (*Minneapolis*)
Famous Barr (*St. Louis*)
Filene's (*Boston and suburbs*)
Garfinckel's (*Washington, D.C.*)
Higbee's (*Cleveland*)
Jordan Marsh (*Boston and suburbs*)
Lord and Taylor (*Boston, Chicago, Dallas, Detroit, Houston, New York, Palm Beach, Washington, D.C.*)
Macy's (*New York*)
Neiman-Marcus (*Atlanta, Bal Harbour, Chicago, Dallas, Ft. Lauderdale, Ft. Worth, Houston, Las Vegas, Miami, San Diego, San Francisco, St. Louis, Washington, D.C., Westchester, NY*)
Nordstrom (*Seattle*)
Rich's (*Atlanta*)
Richard Mann Clothing Company (*Philadelphia*)
Sakowitz (*Dallas, Houston, Midland, Scottsdale*)
Saks Fifth Avenue (*Beverly Hills, Boston, Chicago, Dallas, Kansas City, MO, New York, San Francisco, Stamford, CT, Troy, MI*)
Strawbridge and Clothier (*Philadelphia*)

Books to Help You Build a Better Image
(always to be hidden out of sight)

Color Me Beautiful, Carole Jackson (Acropolis Books, $8.95)

Directory of Personal Image Consultants, (Editorial Services Co. New York, NY, $17.50)

Dress for Success, John Molloy (Warner Books, $3.95)

The Woman's Dress for Success Book, John Molloy (Warner Books, $5.95)

YAP fabrics: Linen, tightly-woven cotton, raw silk, polished silk, wool of all weights, expensive rayon, Gore-Tex (for recreational wear).
Non-YAP fabrics: Double knits, madras, cotton gauze, polished polyester, nylon.

If the Shoe Fits . . .

For the Fast-Track Commute: Nikes

No one knows exactly when women—and some men—started wearing running shoes en route to the office. One story holds that businesswomen began wearing jogging shoes during New York's 1981 transit strike. At any rate, it is now acceptable YAP practice. Your challenge is to find brightly-

To stay in the running for fame and fortune, buy the most expensive joggers you can afford. (The $35 range is a respectable place to start.)

Left: Non-YAP foot favorites for women

Right: A selection for the successfully shod

colored Nikes (and *only* Nikes—no other brand will do) that clash violently with your business suit. The preposterous color combination lets people on the street know you're not actually going to keep those joggers on all day. You are allowed to wear peds (tennis semi-socks), but only if the pompons also clash with the color of your suit or running shoes.

Another challenge is figuring out how to fit your pumps into your stylishly-thin attaché case. (By the way, always change to your pumps in the office restroom. It's tacky to get caught switching footgear in the elevator.)

Primed for Success: the Pump

Some female YAPs believe that pumps earned their name from the throbs of pain they send up and down a wearer's calf. Although boring and miserable to wear, they remain a must for the serious executive woman. Acceptable hues include the ever-exciting brown, black, gray, and beige.

Shoe rules for men:

If you're a man, it's easy to pick the right business shoes. If they sound old-fashioned, those are the ones you want. Good choices: lace-up, wingtip, oxford.

A Ruined Day: The Footgear Faux Pas

"One of my friends on the train told me I wasn't really a professional because the running shoes I wear with my suit in the morning only cost $14. Now I have to get a pair of Nikes."

Left: Men's shoes that look successful in and out of the office

Right: Shoes that can trip you up on the way to the top

Unsuccessful shoes for men:

High-top sneakers, Topsiders, Hush Puppies, Chinese slippers. (Note that Bohemian YAPs, especially entrepreneurs, can sometimes get away with wearing unsuccessful shoes.)

Unsuccessful shoes for women:

Maryjanes, platform shoes, sandals, thigh-high leather boots, spiked high heels (with or without rhinestones).

Prep/Recreational Cross-Dressing

On their days off, many YAPs like to dress like semi-preppies. Recreational dressing and some sports activities are about the only areas of YAP and prep culture that overlap. Thus, leisure YAP dressing includes hiking shorts, Lacoste shirts, chinos, Gore-Tex parkas, and rugby shirts.

Some catalogs from which to order such pseudo-prep gear include Eddie Bauer, L.L. Bean, and Land's End. But remember—as a YAP, you can delve into prep leisure culture only so far. First, you spend a lot more time working than being outdoors. And second, YAPs wouldn't be caught dead in combinations of hot pink and green, madras plaid, or any fabric with whales, ducks, or pheasants on it. YAP is synonymous with suave urban mores, prep with country provincialism. Never the twain shall meet.

Hair: The Long and Short of It

A YAP's first step onto the interview trail usually precipitates his or her initial experience with a hair stylist. Having your hair styled to a shorter length (and for both sexes, short it must be, if you want to succeed) is a traumatic and symbolic moment that no YAP ever forgets. Glance over any YAP's personal photo album. Chances are he or she will be hanging over your shoulder, eager to point out pictures of "when my hair was long."

Fortunately, YAP hair stylists understand this trauma—along with your urge to remain looking "natural" even though you no longer are. These experienced professionals are ready to soothe your insecurities and fill you with enough Chablis so that you are bound to overtip. (Helpful hint: the night before your haircut, do not listen to "Almost Cut My Hair" performed by Crosby, Stills, and Nash on the *Woodstock* album.)

Welcome to Barry Leonard, Crimper.

Have a munchie with our compliments.

☐ Bagel	☐ Coffee
☐ Apple	☐ Tea
☐ Salad	☐ White Wine
☐ Cheese	☐ Red Wine
☐ Yogurt	☐ Hot Chocolate
☐ Pretzels	☐ Iced Tea
☐ Chips	☐ Iced Coffee
☐ Charcuterie	☐ Perrier
☐ _____	
☐ _____	
☐ _____	
☐ _____	

A sample menu offered by one YAP hair salon

A YAP hairstyling salon, complete with bar, personal computer, and digitally-controlled slide show of popular hair styles

Non-YAP hairstylist (also known as a barber)

How to tell if you have found a YAP hair salon:

•Background music is New Wave, classical, or old Beatles tunes.

•The receptionist offers you white wine, cheese, and raw veggies while you wait.

•They use spearmint shampoo.

•Your stylist videotapes your new haircut for future reference.

•The stylists are called "consultants" or "crimpers."

•The person who cuts your hair takes better vacations than you do.

•A haircut costs more than $25, and the price of a perm with tip hovers precariously near the $100 mark.

Avoid places where the stylists are called "barbers," the scissors stick out of disinfectant solution, there are copies of *True Confessions* in waiting areas, and they do not shampoo or blow-dry your hair.

Famous Non-YAP hairstyles in show biz: Sissy Spacek's long tresses in *Carrie*; Louise Lasser's braids in *Mary Hartman, Mary Hartman,* Princess Leia (Carrie Fisher)'s spaced-out 'do' in *Star Wars*.

Selected Items from the Hard-Edged Female YAP's closet

4 blazers

3 summer-skirted suits, 3 winter-skirted suits

10 silk blouses

4 silk dresses

4 hand-knit wool sweaters

2 black-lace "Teddies"
   from Victoria's Secret
5 hand-knit cotton
   sweaters
3 pairs Nikes
2 cotton jogging suits
1 Gore-Tex parka

1 Eddie Bauer down vest
4 pairs dress-for-success pumps
   (black, brown, blue, beige)
1 pair leather boots (for weekend
   art gallery openings)

Selected Items from Bohemian YAP's closet

3 blazers (one Harris Tweed)
2 unlined linen jackets
1 hand-woven nubby purple wool jacket
1 Peruvian shawl
1 Bohemian trying-to-dress-for-success
   suit with too-long skirt, padded
   shoulders, and tapered lines (in purple,
   hot pink, or bright red)
1 Geoffrey Beene jumpsuit
4 Williwear big shirts
5 silk blouses
1 corduroy suit with puffed-sleeve jacket
   and overly-long skirt
4 denim skirts (one with ruffles)
1 purple cotton jogging outfit
1 red Norma Kamali sweatshirt dress
6 hand-knitted wool sweaters, two with illustrations on front
Assorted trousers in wool, denim, and
   khaki
Assorted oxford shirts from Brooks
   Brothers (see YAPtip)
1 full-length Bill Blass down coat

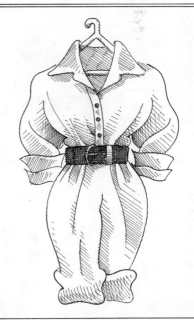

Selected Items from the Late-Bloomer's Closet

2 suits: one, a three-piece pinstripe, the
   other gray flannel
1 seersucker Brooks Brothers suit
2 Pendleton shirts
2 Harris Tweed jackets, one with patches
4 shirts of Scottish plaid cotton, button-
   down collars
6 oxford shirts (assorted blue and white)
2 pairs Wallabees
1 pair Frye boots
2 pairs dress Bass lace-up shoes (burgundy and brown)

3 pairs Lee corduroys (brown, blue, beige)
2 pairs khaki pants

Answer: **Everything but the briefcase!**

48

Stitches in Time: how busy male YAPs can get 5 to 10 minutes extra on the Snooze Alarm each morning:

Wear only black socks, and you won't have any trouble matching them.

Wear only white shirts, so you don't have to think.

YAP females—buy your oxford shirts in the boy's department at Brooks Brothers and save money.

A Woman's Guide to Tying the Knot

Perhaps the psychologists can explain why men still wear long cloth emblems of power and masculinity. We won't even speculate on why women are now donning shorter, knotted versions of the same. The fact remains that in many women's business wardrobes, the necktie is the requisite finishing touch.

Acceptable materials and patterns for knotted ties: Polka dot, foulard, paisley, crepe de chine, raw silk.

Unacceptable tie styles: Bow ties (unless wearing tuxedo-style outfit for evening wear), man-style full-length tie (unless in funky pattern and worn to casual occasion).

A Brief Case Study of Briefcases

Like the value of the dollar, briefcases have been steadily shrinking for some time. By the year 2000, the average attache will measure $4'' \times 5''$, and the retractable handles will descend into an optional Gore-Tex pouch fastened with Velcro.

But forget the future. As a 1980s YAP, your challenge is to make do with the already limited amount of space at hand. The smaller your briefcase, the better. You should be working such outrageous hours that you wouldn't have to carry home any work, anyway. (If you must bring home stacks of papers, conceal them in a Bloomingdale's or Neiman-Marcus shopping bag.)

Women: *Never* carry an attache case plus a handbag. Also, *never* use one of those sissy straps that lets you fling your briefcase over your shoulder.

In selecting a young man's first attache case, we must ask ourselves some very hard questions, such as, how far do we think he's going to go?

Photo Quiz: Which of these are YAP briefcases?

A. Schlesinger Brothers brief, $300
B. Gold-Pfeil Carracciola brief bag, $335
C. Yale leather attache, $80
D. Samsonite attache, $100
E. Garfield lunchbox, $4.49 (thermos included)
F. Ostrich skin attache, $1,650
G. L. J. Hartman briefs, $195 to $230
H. Zero Halliburton gold attache, $320

Answer: B, G, I, J (If you guessed any others, sign up for Tastefulness Training 101.)

Sexy YAP lingerie

If you feel the dress-for-success maxims have squelched your individuality, look to your underwear. Perhaps as a reaction against the rigidity of business dressing, YAP females everywhere are snapping up sexy negligées, garter belts, and camisoles. Josie Cruz Natori, once an investment banker for Merrill Lynch and now a lingerie designer, explains the craze among professionals this way: "If you have to be serious during the day and prove yourself all the time, you want to gratify yourself in the evening. So you can go home and be Cleopatra."

Best catalog for YAP *lingerie*: Victoria's Secret, Box 31442, San Francisco, CA 94131.

*Non-*YAP *lingerie*: Frederick's of Hollywood.

Enjoy the romance. . .

A *luxurious color catalogue of the latest American and European lingerie fashions.* Order yours today!

Victoria's Secret
designer lingerie

Send $3 for a year's subscription of catalogues to Victoria's Secret, Dept. FT-033, Box 31442, San Francisco, CA 94131

Female YAP Jewelry: Pearls of Wisdom
Aside from a tastefully thin watch (to match your tastefully thin waistline), the only acceptable daytime bauble for businesswomen is an elegant string of pearls, worn over a silk blouse and under a jacket. (As for wedding and engagement rings, take a discreet glance around on your first day of work. See if any of the married women have "come out" enough to wear such blatantly sentimental symbols.)

True **YAP** Confessions

My Suit Wasn't Suitable

"As a female Ph.D. in English, I had a rough time trying to get a teaching job in 1980, so I decided to make the switch to the business world by attending the Wharton Alternative Careers program, designed to help liberal arts scholars gain access to corporate jobs.

"My first post-program interview was with a major consulting firm with locations in several cities. I arrived in my new suit, which I thought conformed to all the little rules and regulations my business crash-course had set forth. The young woman interviewing me was about my age and dressed in a blue blazer, white blouse and foulard tie, straight A-line skirt, and pumps. The interview went well, and she offered to refer me to another person in her firm who might have a position available. 'But before you go,' she said, 'I must tell you that you have to get a different suit. You have to be dressed more conservatively and look older. And you have to get different shoes, too.'

"At this, I looked down at my feet and saw that I had made the unpardonable mistake of wearing shoes with rubber soles. Later, more knowledgeable colleagues told me that my blue-striped seersucker suit's padded shoulders and slightly stylish skirt disqualified it as a serious business garment.

"But by then, it was too late—I had no money to buy another suit. Three days later, I took my second interview wearing the same outfit and, needless to say, was never invited back."

White walls aren't just for tires.

A Guide to YAP Living Quarters

Your Home is Your Investment

Owning property is every YAP's dream. You'll want your own place not only for the status involved (no fast-track YAP can brag about a *rented* apartment), but also for the almost magical array of tax breaks that home ownership offers. But why stop at only one apartment or town house? A house in the country enhances one's lifestyle; owning several houses or apartment buildings (to rent to other YAPs) is even better.

The Gentrification Game

The key to becoming a successful real estate entrepreneur (or even just a one-home buyer) lies in picking the right neighborhood in which to invest. Which area of the city is next to be On the Way Up? As rising rents force out the old folks, minorities, and other undesirables, it's up to you—the gentry—to convince other YAPs that this rediscovered neighborhood, where paint strip-

> "I knew the neighborhood was changing when couples came in the store and asked for paint stripper and gloves."
> —Gail Steele, owner of Steele Hardware Store in Brooklyn's Bedford-Stuyvesant section, quoted in National Geographic, June 1983.

per flows in the streets, now features quaint architectural accents and not just aluminum awnings and plaster Madonna statues.

Signs to Look for in Areas On the Way Up:

Gourmet take-out food shops, clothing boutiques (especially vintage clothing stores), sandblasted brick facades, liquor stores with large wine selections, day-care centers with French names, herb gardens, decks on the houses.

Desirable YAP Domiciles

Places to live in the city: rehabbed rowhouses, co-op apartment buildings or condominiums with high ceilings and oak floors, high-tech high rises, converted factory loft buildings, houseboats.

Places to live in the country: farmhouses, converted barns, solar houses, log cabins built from a kit, geodesic domes (Bohemian), beach houses, carriage houses, underground houses.

Places to live in the suburbs (if you must): town house developments, houses costing more than $85,000, starter cottages located in "older" neighborhoods with large trees, a house you design yourself.

NEVER live in: basement apartments, tract houses, converted chicken coops, house trailers, or pre-fab housing.

Y.A.P. tip

Today's slums are sure to be the hot new areas of the 1990s. A cutting-edge investor can pick up bargain town house shells in a city still awaiting gentrification. Prime locations: Camden, NJ; Detroit, MI; Gary, IN; Newark, NJ; South Bronx, NY.

Phrases to question when reading real estate ads

High ceilings: How high is high? Ceilings should be over 8 feet, unless you are reading a special publication for fast-track midgets.

Desirable features: Who, exactly, desires them? Remember that some people *like* marbleized aquamarine countertops.

Historic landmark: Was this where the citywide fire started in 1923?

Lots of possibilities: As an endless source of cocktail party anecdotes, or as a structure to improve?

Needs work, good investment: How much. And how much?

Perfect Starter Town House for Young Professional Couple!

Located in the Renaissance part of town, this little beauty won't last long. 10 ft. ceilings, hardwood floors, skylight, charming rickety spiral staircase, exposed brick, sundeck that overlooks 3 trees. Kitchen with almost-real butcher-block counters, Jenn-Air range, almond refrigerator, built-in wine cellar and ironing board combination. Cappuccino shop on corner. Walk to work—last derelict expelled 3 months ago!

Priced to sell at 5 times what your parents paid for their first home, but you learned all about inflation in your Economics class.

Neighborhoods: What's in a name?

Savvy developers and real estate agents know that YAPs flock to historical neighborhoods. Across the country, entrepreneurs are giving "namelifts" to less-than-desirable areas, based on a loose interpretation of local history.

Original Description	New Name
West of the old abandoned brewery.	Brewerytown
The old Hispanic neighborhood.	Buena Vista.
The old Italian neighborhood.	Belvidere
The rundown part of town, cluttered with burned-out factories.	Olde City
With a view of rotting or charred docks.	Riverview Pier
Surrounds the House of Correction or reformatory.	Inmate Village
Where they used to kill the cows.	Hereford Alley
Where only hicks used to live.	New Town
The street where that guy went crazy and shot 15 people.	Murderer's Nook

The Search for the Perfect Abode

Looking for a place to hang your chapeau? When the real estate agent shows you a home, make sure it has:

- *Lots of natural light*. All YAPs are light freaks. Of course, you're seldom home in the day to appreciate how natural lighting flatters your art collection. But this should not keep you from insisting on places with a superior solar presence.

•*Original or unique features.* When a visitor enters your living quarters, he or she should feel compelled to mention some interesting piece of design that makes your residence dramatic or unusual. These features include spiral staircases, polished wooden floors, skylights, tiled foyers, stained glass, and views of the city or town below. At any self-respecting YAP cocktail party, "original feature" talk can take up at least a half hour.

•*Subtly-shaded walls.* Although white walls are always best, pastels or beige tones will do in a pinch. A YAP's walls should be neutral enough to show slides of the trip to Europe or to soothe a serious case of insomnia.

Original Features to Notice:

High ceilings, interesting moldings, quaint brass doorknockers, leaded glass, oak cabinets; fireplace mantels made of marble, wood or stone; wooden floors, pressed-tin ceilings, wooden beams, tilework in entry halls, industrial elevators (in loft buildings), window seats, spiral staircases.

If your house doesn't have an original feature, buy one in a store.

Unoriginal Features Scorned by YAPs

Panelled rec rooms, wall-to-ceiling mirrors, smoked mirrors, dropped ceilings, brick siding, aluminum awnings, French Provincial steel doors, wall-to-wall shag carpeting, sliding glass doors, flocked wallpaper, asbestos shingles, crystal chandeliers, painted woodwork, linoleum.

Indoor Decor: Fast-Track Lighting and Other Tips

While it is possible to mix and match between these basic YAP decors, sticking with one helps achieve that much-sought-after "designer" look.

The Ingmar Bergman Movie Set: White cotton sofa and chairs; low, light wood coffee tables; rya rugs; Marimekko fabric wallhangings. Track lighting, and *large*, unglazed pottery lamps with pleated white shades. Butcherblock kitchen table, teak dining room table. Kitchen and bathroom tiles in bright blue, brown and orange. Platform beds (Danish bunk beds for the children), light wood dressers with flat surfaces and carved-in handles. Optional: skylight, greenhouse, or metal spiral staircase.

Cozy Country Primitive: Rickety

The Ingmar Bergman Movie Set, or, Sleeptime in Scandinavia

The Cozy, Well-Worn Country-Primitive Look

wide-plank floors, overstuffed chairs, stencilled walls, antique pine or maple furniture with nicks and scratches. Hand-hooked rugs or braided rugs of faded vegetable-dyed wools, quilts as wall-hangings, Windsor chairs with flaking paint, platform rocker. Old oak or brass bed, yellowing lace pillows. Corner cupboard with flaking paint in dining room, fireplace with wooden mantel, exposed wooden beams with nicks and scratches. Faded American primitive paintings with nicks and scratches. Pine table in kitchen, old advertising prints on walls, Hoosier cabinet.

Golden Oak Antique: Oriental rugs, oak floors, oak or mahogany dining room table with caned chairs. Four-poster or high-rise antique bed, watercolors on walls. Bamboo, oak, or brass plant stands with ferns. One piece of whimsical furniture with gargoyle. Clawfoot oak kitchen table, china cabinet with leaded glass panes.

Artsy: Raku pottery on pedestals; low, beige, thickly-woven couch; exposed brick walls. Glass-and-chrome coffee table holding *New Yorker*, *New Republic*, and *American Craftsman*. Handcrafted baskets, modern abstract paintings, wood and metal sculpture. Track lighting, waterbed in master bedroom, futon in guest room.

An accent of golden oak

The Artsy, Pottery-on-a-Pedestal Look

High Tech: Lockers painted red or black, test-tube vases, rolling metal carts. Neon wall hangings, street signs, spray-painted walls. Hospital bed in sleeping loft. In-

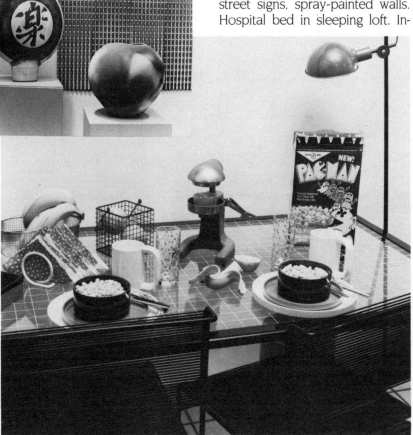

The high-tech breakfast table, complete with video cereal

dustrial kitchen equipment, metal dining room table.

Special sources for decorating tips: *Metropolitan Home* (called *Apart-*

ment Life in its Pre-YAP days), *Architectural Digest* (the YAP decorator's wishbook).

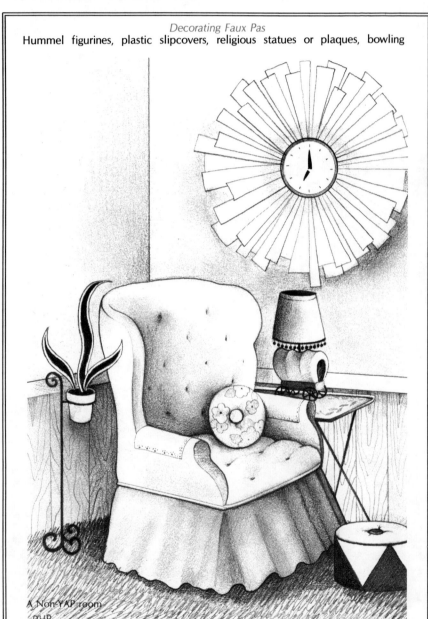

Decorating Faux Pas
Hummel figurines, plastic slipcovers, religious statues or plaques, bowling

A Non-YAP room
PHP

trophies, artificial flowers (not even of silk!), snake plant, portable piano-organ, furniture decorated with the American bald eagle, pool table, built-in bar with tufted vinyl sides, heavy drapes, macrame curtains, East Indian bedspreads, large stuffed animals won at carnivals; copies of the *National Enquirer, Reader's Digest,* or *Us* magazine; plaster statues of deer, ducks, or small Black men; lamps made from gallon wine jugs, Norman Rockwell prints, framed wedding pictures, planters made out of old tires, plastic Christmas wreaths, likeness of Frosty the Snowman or any other pop-culture figure (except Mickey Mouse).

Stripping: The Urge to Expose

YAPs use the Gypsy Rose Lee approach to home improvement: Take it *all* off. Never rest content with whatever "improvements" former tenants or owners may have added to a room: a true YAP wants to strip away any mediocre facade to expose what lies beneath. Often, you'll discover the original chestnut wide-plank floor or the stone fireplace that was hidden behind a wall, and come away from the experience feeling good. But be prepared for the slim chance that the previous owner covered something up for the good reason that it was just plain ugly!

YAP Extras
(to fit into any type of decor)

Computer Room

Recessed lighting and heavy shades prevent glare from computer screen. Ergonomically-designed chairs reduce back and neck strain; special computer stands built of oak (ordered from *Sharper Image* catalog), mounted on casters for easy movement. Up to three computers (depending on size of household).

YAP *personal computers*: IBM, Apple, Commodore.

Non-YAP *personal computers*: Atari, Radio Shack, Timex-Sinclair.

Home Gym

Thick carpeting or foam mats for floor exercises. Soundproofed walls to muffle moans. Free weights or home version of Universal Gym machine, exercy-cle, rowing machine, portable sauna or Jacuzzi, gravity boots (to hang upside-down). *Optional*: VCR to watch Jane Fonda work out.

Greenhouse

Automatic climate control, hydroponic growing system. Sprinkler system, brass faucets in shape of squirrel or duck, brass and oak park bench, laminated copy of *Crockett's Victory Garden*.

YAP *greenhouse plants*: Yellow calla lily, geranium in white or double form with scented foliage, orchids, freesia, staghorn or rabbit's paw ferns, bonsai trees, cherry tomato vines, basil and parsley, crenel-ated cactus over three feet high, amaryllis, tuberose, miniature roses.

Non-YAP *greenhouse plants*: Spider plants, white spathophyllum, red or pink geranium, begonias, coleus, rubber plants, palm trees, aloe, crown of thorns, fig tree (which belongs in living room), ivy, tradescantia (purple passion), Venus flytrap.

Clear the Deck: Outdoor YAP Living

An outdoor deck is a must, especially for urban living. No matter that your redwood paradise overlooks a parking lot—it's your little piece of nature.

Essentials for outdoor spaces: Gas barbecue, white wire furniture, sun umbrella, wooden barrel planters, oak ice bucket, hot tub (climate permitting), oak and brass park bench, and redwood flower boxes.

I Bought Back an Original Feature!

"I came home one day from work and noticed two men standing in front of my town house with a ladder and crowbar, prying a stained glass panel from above my door. Naturally, I panicked. Running into a neighbor's house, I phoned the police. But by the time I got back outside, the men were gone—and so was my leaded glass window.

"Two weeks later, I saw my window in a fine antique shop downtown. After a heated discussion with the antiques dealer, I ended up buying it back at a 10% discount. After all, any other window wouldn't have been the same, and I'm lucky they hadn't shipped it to California or some hick place with even fewer original architectural artifacts, and I never would have found it then! And if I had told the police it was in the shop, they would have confiscated it for evidence. Now I've hired a crime consultant to wire **all** my original features with an alarm system."

YAP Pets: Your Living Accessories

Many YAPs, raised in the suburbs, long for the nostalgic touch a pet provides. If you're childless (as so many YAPs are), pets also provide an easy, inexpensive outlet for parenting instincts.

Dogs were definitely the "in" pets of the '50s and '60s, when lawns were spacious and stay-at-home wives could let Fido out during the day. Now cats have displaced canines as the quintessential fast-track '80s pets. Some veterinarians even limit their practices to felines. Easy to care for (you can leave them for a weekend with a bowl of food and water) and usually less emotionally demanding than dogs, cats are now the stars of numerous humor books and ad campaigns.

Remember to color-coordinate your cat or dog with the furnishings. For example, if your rug and couch are made of white Haitian cotton, *don't* buy a Russian Blue cat. Similarly, those with navy blue Laura Ashley-print settees will want to avoid light-colored dogs like Great Pyrenees.

YAP *cat breeds*: Siamese, Russian Blue, Maine Coon Cat, Persian, Abyssian, Himalayan, assorted good-looking American alley cat types.

Non-YAP *cat breeds*: No such thing.

Essential cat accessories: Scratching post, covered kitty litter pan, basket bed in which cat never sleeps, bat-a-bird, fresh catnip plant, other plants for cat to eat, Kitty Whiz potty-training kit.

YAP *catfood brands*: Nine Lives, Kal Kan, Tender Vittles.

Non-YAP *catfood brands*: Cadillac, store brands, generic brands.

Some YAPs cling to outmoded pets and so must pay the fees of dogwalkers, kennels, and slobber-removal services. If you must have a dog, choose from the following types: Afghan hound, chow, Newfoundland, Alaskan Malamute, golden retriever, long-haired dachshund, small terrier type(Yorkshire, Scottie, Cairn, wire-haired). Single YAPs take note: the more unusual-looking your dog, the more likely that good-looking humans will gravitate toward you in the park.

Non-YAP *dogs*: beagle, basset hound, Weimeraner, poodle, mixed breeds.

Other YAP *pets*: tropical fish (especially salt-water), parrots, mynah birds, horses (at the country place), fantail goldfish, koi, desert tortoises.

Non-YAP *pets*: white mice, gerbils, canaries, hamsters, boa constrictors, tarantulas, painted turtles, tumbling pigeons, parakeets, regular comet-tail goldfish, hermit crab.

True **YAP** Confessions

I Created a Stressful Environment for My Cat

"My cat Jasper started scratching a sore in his ear. I was afraid he might have fleas or mites, so I took him to my veterinarian, who has a downtown practice only for cats. After the vet had examined him for a few moments, she told me that the sore was 'a stress-related illness.' Then she asked if I had broken up with my boyfriend, changed jobs, or moved recently.

" 'Well,' I admitted, 'my roommate and I were talking about moving.'

" 'That's it,' said the vet. 'Jasper must realize something's up, and he's concerned.'

"Until that point, I had held my tongue. But then I got angry. 'The cat just lies around all day—how can that be stressful? If you want stress, I'll give you stress. My job is bananas!'

" 'And obviously,' said the vet, getting smugger as she watched my face get redder and redder, 'you've passed your own stress on to your cat.'

"I went away from her office with instructions to speak in soothing tones and be extra-attentive to Jasper. I can't forget feeling that the vet was attacking me on a personal level—I mean, she made me feel like I was a bad mother!"

For YAPs who transfer stress to animals: The Shaker Heights, Ohio, Board of Recreation offers an adult education class, "Stress Management for Pets."

YAPs Eat Quiche

A Guide to Upscale Food & Drink

YAPs really *do* eat quiche. And gazpacho. And pasta primavera. And paté. Mostly they eat these things while they're out (which they are, almost every day and night of the week). But a few ambitious hobbyists cook that home, too.

Gourmet foods have become the status symbol of the 1980s. Yet YAP food is basically co-opted peasant fare. Black bread, chick peas, pasta—foods that sophisticated people wouldn't be caught dead eating 20 years ago—are really popular in young professional circles. But if you don't come away hungry from the meal, you might not be eating at a genuine YAP restaurant. YAPs relish Italian and Greek food presented in sanitized versions and in much smaller portions than would be served in a real ethnic restaurant. Restaurateurs loosely dub this "nouvelle cuisine" (one male Anti-YAP we know labels it "stingy portions"). In the most extreme cases (some call it "super-nouvelle cuisine"), the restaurant spends more on the garnishes for your entrée than on the main course itself.

All proper YAP fare should be:

•*From another country.* YAPs, who like to travel through their senses, will automatically respect any food with a foreign pedigree. This is known as the "elite edibles" consumption strategy.

Soul-food rib dinner

The same meal as served at a YAP restaurant

•*Ridiculously expensive.* Any food item that costs less than $4.00 per pound has no place in your kitchen cupboard. The YAP cook, like the restaurant-goer, likes to impress guests by providing small portions of delicacies whose total cost could feed a Biafran village for a week. This is known as the "Let them nibble caviar" approach to entertaining.

•*Composed of outlandish ingredients.* YAP cuisine first brought us the hamburger topped with Boursin cheese, deviled eggs with beluga caviar, and fried potato skins stuffed with chili con carne. This is known as the "if you can't feed 'em, confuse 'em" strategy.

•*Incredibly time-consuming to prepare.* YAPs are particularly impressed by any appetizer or entrée that has been pounded, marinated, or stored in some kind of container for hours or days. Another YAP favorite is any entrée or dessert composed of pastry dough that takes four or five years of practice to roll and requires at least seven layers to look good. This is the "quantity time" approach to meal preparation.

An eatery is where working YAPs go to unwind at lunch or dinner. Choose among the following types, and you'll be sure to encounter your own kind:

•*Ye Olde Eatery*: This place usually has an Irish name (Houlihan's, O'Brien's, Gullifty's) or a cutesy-rustic appellation (Rusty Scupper, Hole in the Wall, Hamburger Hamlet, Ground Round, the Railway Depot). Decor consists of reproduced advertising posters, reproductions of old kitchen utensils hanging on the walls, styrofoam tobacco shop statues, oak bar with brass rail, ersatz Tiffany lamps. The oversized menu is chock-full of YAP snack food—quiche, nachos, fried potato skins, spinach salad. The bar specializes in strawberry daiquiris, margaritas, and frosted mugs of beer.

A luncheon interface at Ye Olde Eatery

The trendiest cuisine of the late '80s will be Franco-Japanese, or "Soy meets Béchamel."

Pasta is on the way out (and just when you got that special Cuisinart attachment!). Start reading up on sushi and sashimi (raw fish, Japanese style), which promises to be the newest YAPtrend. (Unfortunately, we have not been able to find a sushi machine to recommend—we're hoping that Williams-Sonoma can import one from Tokyo.)

Appetizers

Carrot Soup 125/200
Chilled Strawberry Soup
Green House Salad 175
hydroponically grown
Fruit Salad 200

Hot Entrees

Cauliflower & Cheddar Quiche 395
Spinach Strudel 400
Quail Stirfry 495
Honey Mustard Chicken 450
Stuffed Eggplant 400
Tempeh Lasagna 450
Licorice Tortellini w/ Mushrooms 450
Omelettes — Boursin 325
Ham & Cheddar
Sea turtle eggs 50¢ extra
◁ $3.00 MINIMUM PER PERSON ▷
BEFORE 130 PM

Sandwiches

Chunky Albacore Salad
Soft Boiled Egg Salad 275
w/ Pinenuts
Roast Beef Tofu
w/ horseradish mayo
Smoked Turkey & Havarti 400
melted on croissant
Corned Beef Special 375
on croissant
Ham & Brie 375
On matzoh
Smoked Turkey 375 *
w/ green mayo
Sushi Burger 595
w/ avocado catsup

*vegetarian

Salads

Caesar Chavez Salad
w/ iceberg lettuce & grapes
Chef's Toss 450
ricotta, prosciutto, anchovies
served on a frisbee
Frosty Pasta 925
Tonnata
Fruit & Cottage Cheese 450
Sausage & Potato
Salad 375

Desserts

Apple Torte Bar
w/ Nabisco 'nilla wafers
Peach Custard Pie
Chocolate Pecan Pie
~~Carrot Cake~~ out
Fig Newton Gelati
Chocolate chip cheesecake
Ki-wi lime Pie
Chocolate Walnut Torte

How to Tell if You Are in a YAP Restaurant

The female *maitre d'* is wearing a tuxedo.
The icewater has a twist of lemon in it.
There are no plates for the bread and butter.
There's no catsup on the table.
The menu is on a blackboard that's hard to see unless you stand up.
Deep-fried brie is on the menu.
The butter is unsalted.
Everything is offered *à la carte*.
There's a tiger lily in the miniature Perrier bottle on your table.
They serve fresh strawberry daiquiris.
Your waiter or waitress has a Ph.D. in English.
They serve avocado omelets at brunch.
The bar has potted plants on it.
The owner is a former college professor of yours.
Your plate of quiche and salad arrives garnished with kale and
    a slice of orange.
The bathroom sink holds a bar of lavender Crabtree & Evelyn soap.

•*The Gourmet Cafeteria*: Goodbye, Horn and Hardart! For busy YAPs who must work late at the office, these types of fast-food establishments provide sleek ambience, color-coordinated trays and napkins, and alstroemeria lilies on the tables. Pick up a carafe of Chablis along with an array of salads, stirfrys, and country patés for easy consumption.

On line at the local gourmet cafeteria

The Elegantly Understated Restaurant, in all its tastefulness

•*Elegantly Understated Surroundings*: Everything here is ordered *à la carte*, and the entrées start at $9.95 (for a pasta dish). Butcherblock tables with elegant, heavy cotton place mats or mauve table cloths with flowered napkins coordinate with the walls and moldings, usually painted in tastefully juxtaposed colors. Favorite color combinations: mauve and gray, gray and tangerine, off-white and light pink, and blue and beige.

The Nouvelle Experience
(YAP *food staples*)

Black bread, hummous, baba ganoush (eggplant paste), Greek *spanikopita* or anything made with filo dough, pesto (paste made from basil leaves), black bean soup, unsalted butter, romaine lettuce and endive, anchovies, monkfish, tortellini, puff pastry, dips, flatbreads, Perrier, sparkling cider (Martinelli's), Bloody Marys, spinach lasagna, boursin cheese, gazpacho, quiche, brie, deep-fried brie, fried potato skins with exotic toppings, nachos, chicken salad with white seedless grapes, fresh fruit salads, croissants (filled and plain), sandwiches served on croissants, asparagus, brioche, artichokes, mustard vinaigrette, omelets filled with odd stuff such as lox or stir-fried vegetables, poached salmon, potato salad made with new potatoes still in their skins, avocados (especially in combination with other ingredients), bean sprouts (crossover from hippie culture), fresh herbs, Pepperidge Farm cookies, antipasto salads, Godiva chocolates, Haägen-Dazs ice cream, crepes,

A Typical YAP's Workday Diet

BREAKFAST—Almond croissant. English breakfast tea *or* coffee made in a Melitta. (Consumed at home or at the café around the block from the office.)

LUNCH—Sandwich of roast lamb and sun-dried tomatoes on onion rye with horseradish mayonnaise and romaine. Five-ounce bottle of Martinelli's sparkling cider. (Both consumed at desk—too busy to get away.)

DINNER—Order of oriental-style scallops with snow peas purchased at gourmet take-out and heated in microwave. Side order of brown and wild rice with mushrooms. Glass of Mondavi white wine. (Consumed at dining room table while looking over papers.)

The YAP Vegetable Manifesto:
We Will Serve Every Cooked Vegetable Before Its Time

Thanks to YAP restaurateurs and cooking schools, a diner is hard-pressed to ever taste a vegetable that's actually *cooked.* When admiring the veggies at a YAP table, "crunchy and crispy" are proper adjectives to use. Another popular descriptive phrase is "delicate flavor."

If you are a YAP, you're probably already used to hearing your parents say, "The broccoli is underdone!" Ignore them, or show them a Craig Claiborne column. This is your chance to get even for all the mushy canned peas, spinach, and creamed corn they made you eat when you were growing up. If they wear dentures, it will only make your revenge all the sweeter.

---

snow peas (especially stuffed), carrot cake, sushi, wild rice, red lettuce, kiwi fruit.

YAP Junk Food
(any food Mom used to serve you)

Mashed potatoes, cole slaw, blintzes, pot roast, meat loaf, macaroni and cheese, french fries (unless they're cottage fries), rice pudding, Wienerschnitzel, sauerkraut (unless on a Reuben), gefilte fish, Wonder Bread, matzoh, corned beef and cabbage, frozen peas, Oreos, Fig Newtons, open-face turkey sandwiches on white bread, chicken soup, stewed tomatoes, chicken pot pies, ice cream cake (Carvel's), rice pudding, white bread, canned corn, margarine, instant coffee, eggnog from a carton, frozen pizza, fried chicken, beef stew, Aunt Jemima frozen waffles, iceberg lettuce, baked beans, canned spinach, stewed prunes, pork chops, hot dogs, Baco Bits, marshmallows, chocolate pudding, Campbell's tomato soup, Cup-a-Soup, Hamburger Helper, spaghetti and meatballs, chicken and rice, onion dip made with dried onion soup mix, Jell-O.

Extra-virgin olive oil, 1 liter, $14.50

1-pound bag of Bloomingdale's Tanzania Kilimanjaro coffee beans, $5.00

Can of Hungarian paprika, 5 ounces, $2.25

1-pound bag of Bloomingdale's decaffeinated Swiss chocolate almond coffee, $6.25

12½-ounce tin of Bremner Wafers, $5.50

Abbott's Seafood Chowders, five 8-ounce cans, $11.50

Crabtree & Evelyn sea salt, 8.8 ounces, $3.50

Ancel chocolate mousse mix, 3 ounces, $2.75

Select Origins™ "French Essentials" — thyme, tarragon, and rosemary, $11.50

Fortnum & Mason's Harvey's Sauce (instead of Worcestershire), 6 ounces, $3.50

Crabtree & Evelyn walnut oil, 17.6 ounces, $9.75

London Herb & Spice Co. chamomile tea, 25 sachets, $2.50

Texarkana Collection burgundy jelly, $6.50

Madagascar green peppercorns, 2 ounces, $1.75

Fini balsamic vinegar, 3.2 ounces, $12.50

Pilcarone Dijon mustard, 3½-ounce tube, $1.90

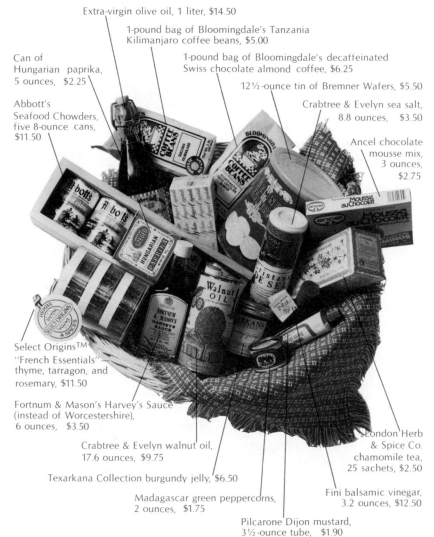

A basket of food staples for the YAP housewarming

72

How To Convert Your Refrigerator and Cupboard

Existing Food Item	Price	Replace with	Price
Skippy Peanut Butter	1.33	Imported Chestnut Cream	3.95
Wonder Bread	.69	a dozen croissants	9.60
Heinz white vinegar	.73	tarragon or basil vinegar	4.00
Oreo cookies	1.79	hand-packed Oreo ice cream	3.50
1 lb. hamburger	1.35	1 lb. veal	7.59
flour and eggs	1.84	4 orders stuffed crepes from gourmet cookshop	14.00
bottle of seltzer	.34	bottle of Perrier	1.80
iceberg lettuce	.69	romaine	1.40
Wesson cooking oil	.99	walnut oil	9.50
Smucker's raspberry jam	1.39	Silver Palate's "It's the Berries"	9.00
1 lb. Velveeta	2.09	1 lb. Brie	5.49
Realemon juice	.87	6 lemons	1.50
Ritz crackers	1.49	Norwegian flatbread	1.70
1 lb. Maxwell House	2.92	1 lb. espresso	4.40
Carolina white rice	.63	½ lb. wild rice	7.50
can of Reddiwhip	1.29	3 pints whipping cream	2.40
Mrs. Paul's fish filets	2.29	1 lb. swordfish steaks	7.99
McCormack's Italian spices	1.07	windowsill herb garden	14.00
French's mustard	.49	Mustard Pommery	3.70
Ragú spaghetti sauce	.93	1 pint marinara sauce from gourmet take-out	1.69
Ronzoni Spinach Noodles	.65	½ lb. fresh pasta	2.50
Box of Lipton Tea bags	.59	Twining's Earl Grey	2.55
Total	$26.45	Total	$116.76

Chocolate, Ice Cream, and Popcorn: The Three Favorite YAP Munchies

Healthy as nouvelle cuisine is, some YAPs still get cravings for things that aren't exactly nutritious. But you can assuage your sense of guilt by restricting your pigouts to *gourmet* snacks. A real YAP knows the *best* places to get such munchies, and will defend his or her choice of snacking spots. "This is good, but it's not quite as good as the ice cream at Harry's" is required commentary when sampling goodies in cities or neighborhoods other than your own.

The chocolate you eat should be from Switzerland, or at least have a European name. YAPs are going wild for the new flavors of gourmet popcorn—nacho, banana, pizza, grape, and chocolate—popping up in trendy shopping centers. (Remember, it was YAPs who made Oreo ice cream a standard flavor.) In fact, any disgusting junk food from your youth, such as Reese's Pieces, chocolate-covered raisins, or Ringdings, becomes a fashionable dessert if mashed down into vanilla ice cream.

YAP penny candy

A *Select* List of YAP Ice Cream Parlors and Gelateria

BOSTON
Emack and Bollo, 290 Newbury Street
Steve's, 191 Elm Street (Somerville, MA)

NEW YORK CITY
Heaven, 836 Ninth Avenue
Peppermint Park, 1225 First Avenue

WASHINGTON, D.C.
Bob's Famous, 2416 Wisconsin Avenue

DENVER
The Apple Tree Ice Cream Parlor, 3250 Youngfield, (Applewood, CO)

PHILADELPHIA
Hillary's (three locations)

SAN FRANCISCO
Double Rainbow, 1653 Polk Street

SEATTLE
Procopio, 1501 Western Avenue

ATLANTA
Steve's Homemade, 1172 Peachtree Street

Y.A.P. tip

Need an unusual gift for a friend? Chocolate Photos, a New York firm, uses photographs to make chocolates that resemble people. Imagine your friend's surprise when he opens up a package filled with little cocoa replicas of his face! You supply the photo—a box of a dozen chocolate portraits costs $22.50.

| Good | Better | Best (this model hooks up to pasta attachment) | Automatic pasta attachment (add it to your Christmas list) | Ostentatious (at over $300, more suited to restaurants) |

The Cuisinart Hierarchy

The YAP's Fantasy Kitchen: A Quiz

How many of these items do you own?

□ industrial stove
□ Cuisinart or Robot Coupe food processor
□ wok
□ Farberware pots, Dansk enamelled pots, or Calphalon cookware
□ salad spinner
□ mushroom brush
□ cloth bag for salad greens
□ garlic cellar
□ garlic press
□ marble pastry board
□ windowsill herb garden
□ Italian cappuccino and espresso maker
□ crêpe pan
□ mortar and pestle
□ soufflé dish
□ artichoke plates
□ tortilla press
□ English muffin rings
□ spring-base cheesecake pan
□ fish poacher
□ asparagus steamer
□ French Croque Monsieur toasting iron
□ hand-crank pasta machine
□ electric pasta machine
□ rolling butcherblock cart
□ Gelato ice cream machine from Italy

□ kitchen scale
□ omelet pan
□ bacon press
□ egg rings
□ high-speed potato baker
□ electric flour mill
□ electric juicer
□ pizza brick
□ soda syphon (makes seltzer out of water)
□ pepper mill
□ Belgian waffle iron
□ electric potato peeler
□ Sabatier or Henkel knives
□ professional ice cream scoop

(Give yourself one point for each item checked off)

25 *to* 40: Congratulations! you are well on your way to the YAP's dream kitchen.

15 *to* 24: You have a way to go, but you've made a stab in the direction of Sabatierland.

10 *to* 14: If you rush subscription forms to *Gourmet* and *Bon Appétit* today, there's still hope.

10 *and below*: You're probably still eating Chef Boyardee ravioli, cold. From the can.

Non-YAP Kitchen Appliances

Crockpot	Dazey Seal-a-Meal
Presto Hotdogger	canning equipment
Deep-Frier	Ginzu knife sets
Mr. Coffee coffeemaker	Teflon-coated frying pan
Amazing Vegomatic Slicer (sold on late-night TV)	

We gave a YAP couple a 5-minute shopping spree in Bloomingdale's Housewares Department. Choosing from Bloomie's state-of-the-art selection of kitchen gadgets, they were able to come close to their fantasy kitchen.

YAP Kitchen Quiz Part 2

Look again at the list of kitchen items. How many have you used in the last 6 months?

25 *to* 40: Have you been on a leave of absence? Maternity leave? Are you sure you're a YAP?

15 *to* 24: You don't work many weekends, do you?

10 *to* 14: You threw at least 2 dinner parties last season.

10 *and below*: Make sure your cleaning lady takes care of the Cuisinart: dust isn't good for the motor.

Eat, Drink, and Be YAPpy

While not as drink-obsessed as they are food-fixated, YAPs have very strong feelings about what beverages and liqueurs to imbibe.

Non-alcoholic YAP beverages: Sparkling cider, Perrier, V-8, herbal iced tea, iced tea made from Twining's, espresso, Tab (*always* with lemon), fresh-squeezed orange juice, fresh-squeezed lemonade.

Non-YAP soft drinks: Mountain Dew, Hawaiian Punch, Kool-Aid, milk, tap water, instant coffee, hot chocolate, Postum, Ovaltine, canned iced tea, Gatorade, Dr. Pepper, any orangeade from a soda fountain.

YAP *liquors and liqueurs*: It is not acceptable in YAP circles to get rip-roaring drunk. One never knows when a contact is going to pay off, so, to avoid ruining networking possibilities, it is best to refrain from getting sloshed. Drink excessive amounts of alcohol only in the privacy of your home while watching a tape of *Kramer vs. Kramer* on the VCR.

Hard Liquors: In the last few years, YAPs have been gravitating toward Scotch as the hard drink of choice. Acceptable brands include Chivas Regal and Glenlivet. If you must drink vodka, stick to Stolichnaya. Jack Daniels is the only sour mash whiskey permissible, and appropriate bourbons include Wild Turkey and Rebel Yell (on sale only in Kentucky).

Acceptable mixed drinks: Gin and tonic, vodka martini, Bloody Mary.

Marginal "sissy" drinks (popular with female YAPs): kirs, daiquiri (especially frozen strawberry type), margarita, Black Russian, Manhattan.

Non-YAP mixed drinks: Rum and coke, pina colada, screwdriver (except at brunch), Harvey Wallbanger, Purple Jesus, Singapore Sling.

The YAP Cult of Wine

The true YAP is an oenophile who has taken a wine-tasting course, knows his way around basic European grapes, and dreams of taking a trip to the Napa Valley to visit all those wineries. Buying wine by the case for home consumption is *de rigeur*, and some wealthy YAPs consider buying a small winery in an out-of-the-way

Non-YAP wines (Chateau Ausone doesn't *need* 30-second spots by Stiller and Meara.)

place such as Indiana, Idaho, or Virginia. (See "YAP Second Careers," p. 37.)

The very best YAP wine is one which your friend has never heard of but you know all about. However, pressed for popular labels and (for picnics and large parties), a recommendation for good jug wine, a YAP can oblige.

Sure-bet California YAP wineries

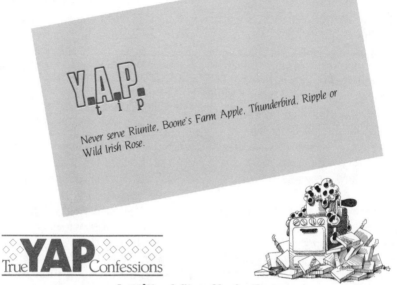

Y.A.P. tip

Never serve Riunite, Boone's Farm Apple, Thunderbird, Ripple or Wild Irish Rose.

True **YAP** Confessions

A Hill of Stouffer's Beans

"About a year before there were any gourmet cookshops in our town, my boss was giving a Christmas party at her weekend country place. She called me up and told me that she was very busy doing a special project—would I do a favor for her and call up all the area supermarkets and find out which one had fifteen packages of Stouffer's Green Beans with Mushrooms? She emphasized that no other brand would do.

"It took me all morning to find a store with fifteen packages of the stuff, and most of the frozen-food managers acted as if I was crazy. When I finally picked them up, I had to endure the stares of the other customers as I left with two bags stuffed with frozen beans. I spent more than $20 of the company's petty cash on those gourmet legumes!

"Later that night at the party, my boss basked in the warmth of compliments about her great home cooking. I still don't know where she stowed all the empty Stouffer's boxes. I often think I'd have been spared if only she could have gotten fresh-cooked green beans delivered to her door."

(for moderately priced wine): Robert Mondavi, Beringer, Korbel (for champagne), Inglenook, Los Hermanos.

Non-YAP American Wineries: Gallo, Manischewitz, Taylor, Christian Brothers.

After the Carrot Cake: YAP Liqueurs

No fine meal is complete without the after-dinner drink. Here are some suggestions for the perfect YAP nightcap.

YAP liqueurs: B&B, Framboise, Remy Martin, Courvoisier, Cointreau, Grand Marnier, Drambuie.

Non-YAP liqueurs: Blackberry brandy, Amaretto, Tia Maria, Jacquin's Triple Sec, Bols, Kahlua.

Some YAP Cookbooks

New York Times Cookbook, James Beard, Moosewood (Bohemian YAP), The Silver Palate Cookbook, Vegetarian Epicure (Bohemian).

Non-YAP: Better Homes and Gardens, Betty Crocker, Fanny Farmer, Diet for a Small Planet.

Gourmet Foods to Go: Store-Bought Haute Cuisine

However well-equipped the kitchen, a hectic schedule leaves many YAPs with little time to spend there. Devoting three hours to the latest recipe from Bon Appétit must, unfortunately, be relegated to the weekend. During the work week, what's a gourmet YAP to do?

The last few years have seen the advent of what Chicago entrepreneur Jeffrey Nemetz calls "the specialty cuisine retail movement." The rise of the gourmet take-out establishment has sounded the death knell for pizza joints and Chinese monosodium glutamate outlets all over the country. For the price of a decent restaurant meal, the busy YAP can choose from fresh salads, sandwiches, and entrées such as roast honey duck, salmon en croute, and Coquille St. Jacques, all to go.

Most gourmet take-out emporiums view their typical customer as "the young professional—single or attached. And generally we see the same faces three or four times a week," says Gregory Conocchioli, co-owner of What's Cooking in Philadelphia. Because of the large number of dual-career YAP couples, another gourmet entrepreneur views such establishments as just right "for people who care about the quality of their convenience."

"It changed my style of life," says a Bohemian YAP antiques dealer. "Before, I shopped and cooked. Now, every night, I buy my dinner half a block away. The food is superb, wonderfully varied—and I see them cooking it, so it's really not like buying it from a store at all. It's like they're cooking for their friends."

DDL Foodshow — The King Kong of YAP Takeout

Founded by movie producer Dino De Laurentiis, this 12,000-square-foot haven for YAP gluttons is patterned after emporiums like Fauchon in Paris and Peck in Milan. Like its founder's remake of *King Kong,* it is larger than life, featuring a soaring atrium skylight, theatrical track lighting and standup brass espresso bar. Gael Green describes it as "probably the most stunningly handsome grocery in the world, certainly New York."

Chic Munchies by Mail

Looking for something special to send friends at Christmas, or as gifts to business associates? Scores of gourmet mail-order companies can help you send fresh *foie gras,* baby artichokes, chili wreaths, and caviar to people on your list (even to friends who insist on living miles from the nearest sushi bar). Or order some goodies for yourself — you deserve it!

Some sample mail-order delectables:

Chocolate truffles, some filled with Champagne, arrive from Switzerland several times a week. Prices range from $13.50 for 9 ounces to $51 for 36 ounces. Available at *Teuscher Chocolates of Switzerland,* 620 Fifth Avenue, New York, NY 10020. Tel. (212) 246-4416.

Chili wreaths made of the dried red peppers essential to Mexican cuisine are $25, plus $10 shipping costs, from *Herman Valdez Fruit Stand,* P.O. Box 116, Velarde, NM 87582. Tel. (505) 852-2129.

Foie Gras marinated in Cognac or truffle juice and packed in a porcelain goose can be shipped overnight anywhere in the U.S. for only $165. Order from *Balducci's,* 424 Sixth Avenue, New York, NY 10009. Tel. (212) 673-2600.

Golden Whitefish Caviar may not be as glamourous as the Russian stuff, but at $47 for ten ounces, it makes a respectable mail-order gift. *California Sunshine Fine Foods,* 2171 Jackson St., San Francisco, CA 94115. Tel. (415) 567-8901.

Water Buffalo-Milk Mozzarella At $10.50 per pound, this cheese erases all memories of the gloppy pizza-topping version. From *Todaro Brothers Mail Order,* 555 Second Avenue, New York, NY 10016. Tel. (212) 679-7766.

Artichokes are available year round from Castroville, CA (the Artichoke Capital of the World). Order an assortment with 160 extra small, 72 small, 42 medium, or 24 large for $50 east of the Mississippi, $40 west. ($25 for California residents.) *Giant Artichoke,* 11241 Merritt St., Castroville, CA 95012. Tel. (408) 633-2778.

Remember to tell the companies to ship to your office or your friend's office. (You know you'll never be home when the goodies arrive.)

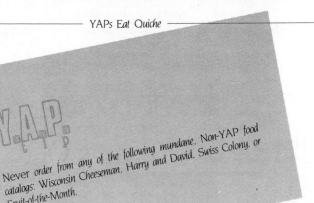

Never order from any of the following mundane, Non-YAP food catalogs: Wisconsin Cheeseman, Harry and David, Swiss Colony, or Fruit-of-the-Month.

A Select List of YAP Gourmet Take-out Joints

New York, NY:
Dean & DeLuca, 121 Prince Street
Neuman & Bogdonoff, 1385 Third
 Avenue
Pasta & Cheese, 1896 Broadway
The Silver Palate, 274 Columbus
 Avenue
SoHo Charcuterie, 195 Spring Street
Self-Chef, 1224 Lexington Avenue
Word of Mouth, 1012 Lexington
 Avenue
Zabar's, 2245 Broadway
E.A.T., 1064 Madison Avenue

Washington, DC:
Fete Accomplie, 3714 Macomb Street
 NW
Sutton Place Gourmet, 3201 New
 Mexico Avenue NW
Suzanne's, 1735 Connecticut Avenue
 NW

Philadelphia:
Public Cookshop, 1630 Pine Street
Moveable Feast, 4443 Spruce Street
Day by Day, 2101 Sansom Street
The Market at the Commissary, 130 S.
 17th Street
What's Cooking?, 263 S. 15th Street

Atlanta:
Proof of the Pudding, 980 Piedmont
 Avenue

Boston:
The Fishmonger, 252 Huron Avenue,
 Cambridge
Formaggio, 81 Mt. Auburn Street,
 Cambridge

Chicago:
Zambrana's, 2344 N. Clark Street
Kenessey Gourmets, 403 W. Belmont
Mitchell Cobey Cuisine, 100 East Walton
 Street
A La Carte, 1229 Greenbay Road
 (Wilmette, IL)
Anything Goes, 2256 N. Clark Street
La Salle Street Market, 745 N. La Salle
 Street
Beautiful Food, 546 Chestnut (Winnetka,
 IL)

Princeton, N.J.:
La Cuisine, 183C Nassau Street
Dave's Pasta Pick-up (Princeton
 Junction)

San Francisco
Vivande, 2125 Fillmore Street
Neiman-Marcus Oppenheimer, Epicure
 Department, 2050 Divisadero Street
Say Cheese, 856 Cole Street

Phoenix:
Marche Gourmet, 6166 N. Scottsdale
 Road

Los Angeles:
Hugo's, 8401 Santa Monica Boulevard
Le Grand Buffet, 9527 Santa Monica
 Boulevard
Tutto Italica Delicatezza, 8657 Sunset
 Boulevard

Seattle:
Your Place Or Mine, 34th and Union

Reach out and touch a contact

Finding people and finding time

While networking with fellow YAPs, your greatest challenge is *communication*. How to stay in touch when everyone you know is working crazy hours, flying off to places at a moment's notice, or spending weekends at the country place? Fortunately, modern technology offers several solutions to this dilemma:

•*The Phone-Answering Machine.* An essential accouterment for the YAP household. Several years ago, only Amtrak and downtown movie theaters used them. Now mechanical message-takers have supplanted the live answering service as the status emblem for the busy careerist. Through the miracle of electromagnetic tape, your voice apologizes for your absence, urges your caller to speak following the beep, and promises you'll "get back" real soon.

Advantages: The machine ensures your round-the-clock availability to friends and business associates (*if* they wait for the beep). On most models, you can change your recording daily to show callers how clever you are. Some machines let you screen incoming calls while you're home, too. (You'll like listening to your friends speak in a pompous, stilted manner, stumbling over their words as they answer your disembodied request for a concise message.)

Disadvantages: The machine also

makes you electronically available to your mother, who can call and leave messages that begin, "Remember me?" or "I know you're too *busy* to call home, but . . ." You also get some of the most interesting obscene phone calls you've ever heard from a new breed of pervert who's into delayed gratification.

•"*Call-Waiting*" *Service*. This "must have" phone accessory enables you to prioritize calls and place people on hold indefinitely. The technology allowing you to dump somebody when a more important person in your network calls used to be available only at work—and then only if you had a personal secretary. Now enjoy that degree of phone power in the privacy of your own home.

Advantages: You won't miss important job offers just because you've been on the phone all evening with a friend. If you're bored with a conversation, make a clicking sound with your tongue and tell the person you have another call.

Disadvantages: Mom again! Unless you are keeping two people on hold, your line is never officially "busy." This means that your mother can call you during *any* phone conversation.

Other YAP phone fundamentals:

•*Call-Forwarding Service*. For the traveling YAP, this service directs phone calls to wherever you are, and keeps burglars from knowing you're not home.

•*Long-Distance Service*. Your network is long-distance, so why pay Ma

A selection of beautifully-designed phones

83

Bell for all those lengthy heart-to-hearts? Admittedly, a smaller company's connections sometimes make you feel like you're back in the schoolyard playing "telephone," but it beats considering a second mortgage every time your phone bill arrives. Choose MCI, Sprint, IT&T or a competitor, but *never* pay retail for tying up cross-country phone wires.

The Cult of the Phone

Every YAP *owns* his or her telephones. If you're still renting, get with it! Even if your abode has only four or five rooms, you need three or more extensions. And they can't just be run-of-the-mill sets. There's a certain aesthetic code: telephones must be superior in design, technological achievement, and sound (with at least three different rings). Choose at least one of each of the following types:

- *The Memory Phone.* Doesn't remind you where your keys are, but *does* allow you to dial frequently-called numbers by pushing one button. Also re-dials busy numbers.
- *The Secret Agent Phone.* Comes equipped with a special code so that only people who know it can reach you. Great for keeping nosy family members at a distance.
- *The Cordless Phone.* Allows you to wander around aimlessly or work out on your rowing machine with no cords attached.
- *The Bathroom Phone.* Helps you make use of every precious moment and avoid the embarrassment of being indisposed when that important call comes.
- *The Beautifully Designed Phone.* Has won awards for its great looks; may be in a museum collection. Makes you feel sophisticated every time you use it.
- *The Novelty Phone.* Mickey Mouse and Snoopy are a bit passé, so try to find something *unique*. (Latest rage is the Duck Decoy phone in The Sharper Image.)
- *The Cleverly-Concealed Phone.* Ugly plastic parts are hidden away in a sleekly-finished wooden case that blends perfectly with your decor.

Y.A.P.

Pick a ring that sings.
Your phone's sound is just as important as its looks, and you can't judge that from a catalog. Check with friends before buying. One YAP male we know bought an Italian-designed phone with a "come-hither" ring: "It *doesn't* nag, it purrs."

YAP to a friend answering the phone: "Gee, I was waiting for the beep—I've called three people today, and you're the first *real* person I've talked to!"

The Hierarchy of Phone-Answering Machines

All phone machines are *not* created equal. The best ones have:

- A remote pager that lets you listen to your messages on a phone away from home.
- A shut-off device so that the machine doesn't record the sound of the dial tone when your callers hang up in disgust.
- A dual cassette system so you can easily change outgoing messages.

Answering Machine Etiquette

1. Don't bore your callers with an interminable, cutesy, poetic greeting you think is *très* witty. This goes double for a machine that greets callers with a few bars of jazz or mood music—which only gives them a longer wait before the beep and makes them wonder if they've been placed on hold.

2. Are you living with someone of the opposite sex? Trying to hide it from business associates and other busybodies? *Don't* leave one of those bland messages that say something like, "You have reached 555–9969." It's a dead giveaway. Instead, get two phone lines and *two* machines.

3. *Never* sing on your message tape.

4. *Never* do an impression of Cary Grant, Jimmy Durante, Mae West, or Clark Gable on your message tape. (One journalist used to have Gordon Liddy, Timothy Leary, and other distinctive media personalities record answering messages for him. But who would actually *believe* they were the real McCoy?)

5. Never leave a message you

Ours was a Phone Machine Romance

"I answered a guy's personal ad with a letter and photograph and included my phone number. I go to a lot of night meetings, and I'm seldom home 'til after 11 P.M. So one night I came home, switched on the phone machine, and heard one of the funniest, most interesting messages ever. It was this guy, leaving his phone number!

"I called him back, and left a message on **his** answering machine. After that, we went back and forth on tape for the next two weeks. By the time I actually met Keith, it felt like we were old friends, and we've been dating ever since."

85

wouldn't want your mother to hear. Sooner or later, she will.

6. Callers: Resist the urge to leave enigmatic messages that may confuse or panic the recipient. (*Beep.* "Uh, hi—this is Dave. There's something I wanted to tell you but (*muffled sobs*), uhhh, oh my God! . . ." *Click.*)

7. Callers: Never break up with a lover or fire someone on tape.

Beepers: The Cutting-Edge Craze

For a greater range of accessibility than even answering machines provide, try a paging beeper. A few years ago, a beeper sounding in a crowded movie theater or concert hall was most likely beckoning a doctor. But an increasing number of people are using remote pagers to keep track of family members. One pregnant YAP used a beeper to track down her executive husband when she was going into labor. Parents we know attach one to their teenage daughter to enforce curfews. We predict that in the next two years, personal pagers will become YAP necessities.

The Omnipresent Datebook

The obsession to keep in touch with contacts fuels another YAP passion—time management. No self-respecting YAP would be caught dead without his or her pocket-size datebook outlining

Two styles of pocket calendars: *Left:* regular *Right:* Bohemian

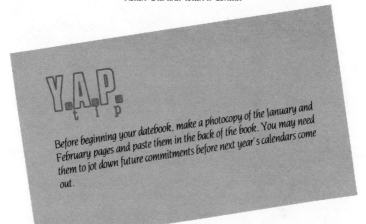

Y.A.P. tip

Before beginning your datebook, make a photocopy of the January and February pages and paste them in the back of the book. You may need them to jot down future commitments before next year's calendars come out.

daily, weekly, and monthly commitments. Before making a date over the telephone with a business associate or friend, always be sure to say, "Let me check my calendar" even if you don't have it with you. Upon finding a free slot of time, the proper phrase is, "Okay, I'm pencilling you in." This keeps the listener in suspense as to whether the date will be erased if something better comes along.

The style of the datebook varies considerably from one type of YAP to another. A leather book is best, of course, but vinyl give-away types are perfectly acceptable. One Bohemian YAP we know (They're always *so* original!) makes up her own datebook as she goes along on separate sheets of colorful paper.

Another Time Accessory: The Very Visible Watch

To show that you are very concerned with time and all that it means, you must wear a watch expensive enough to be insured. "A designer label can be hidden,"

says fashion sociologist Anne Hollander in *Savvy* magazine, "but a watch, recognizable by its design, thinness, and degree of gold . . . immediately speaks of money." If possible, wear a readily recognizable brand, such as Rolex.

However tempted you are to know what time it is at every second of the day, avoid those tacky watches that beep every fifteen minutes. They remind people of egg timers.

The Ultimate YAP Maxim: Time Is Money, or You Can Get Good Help These Days

YAPs don't have spare time. In order to get the *quality time* necessary for your work and personal life, you'll need to hire people to do everything you can't get around to doing, including watering your plants, cleaning your house, raising your kids, walking your dog, visiting your parents, cooking your meals, and locating attractive members of the opposite sex for you to date.

Photo Quiz: Can you guess which watches a YAP would wear?

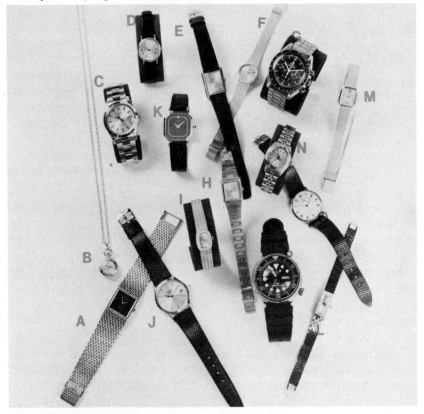

Answer: YAP watches are C, D, E, F, G, H, J, M, N, O, and P.
Non-YAP watches are A, B, I, K, and L.

The *details:*

A. 18k gold Baume Mercier quartz watch, $5,300. *Elegant, but too gangsterish to appeal to YAPs.*

B. Colibri gold-plated pendant watch, $79.50. *Much too cute and feminine.*

C. Men's Rolex, $1,970. *The favorite of many YAPs.*

D. Women's Concord, $390. *A perfect timepiece to start with.*

E. Men's tank-style Concord, $390. *Another perfect starter.*

F. Women's gold-tone Seiko, $350. *A respectable watch for any beginning achiever.*

G. Omega Speedmaster Professional Moon Watch, $530. *Flight-qualified for all manned space flights, and the first wristwatch on the Moon. Perfect conversation piece for YAP parties.*

H. Seiko women's quartz, $225. *Another starter.*

I. Women's Baume & Mercier diamond bezel, $2,950. *The price is right, but much too gaudy.*

J. Men's 14k gold Concord quartz, $1,390. *An excellent choice.*

K. Men's Seiko Lasalle quartz, $295. *With its black face, a trifle too mysterious-looking.*

L. Women's Baume & Mercier diamond bezel, $2,700. *Much too ostentatious.*

M. Women's Seiko sport watch, $225. *Another good starter watch for leisure hours.*

N. Women's Rolex Oyster Perpetual, $1,725. *Excellent!*

O. Concord 9-Line, $490. *4 millimeters thick; thin is best.*

P. Seiko quartz diver's watch, $350. *A must for those business trips to the Caribbean.*

Help for Female SuperYAPs (and some male YAPs, too)

In 1982, former writer and consultant Alison Scott founded the Support System, a personal lifestyle consulting firm, because "you don't want to give up being a decent person, seeing friends and cooking dinners, but you have other things to do, too." The Support System helps busy YAPs do anything they don't have time to do, including entertaining, buying a wardrobe, waiting for appliances to be delivered, buying gifts, getting artwork framed, housecleaning, researching vacation spots, planting gardens, and finding pieces of furniture.

One YAP hired the Support System to buy two large plants to camouflage the stereo speakers that overwhelmed his living room. In the course of a few months, Scott's staff also researched time-sharing condominiums in the Republic of Ireland, helped another client decide between leasing and buying a car, and bought wedding presents on behalf of several busy male YAPs.

One popular service the firm offers is the "charity run"—an employee comes to a YAP's house, picks up old clothes and flotsam, delivers them to a charity of the YAP's choice, and returns with a receipt good for a tax deduction. Says Scott, "If young executives are in the 50% tax bracket, the $15.00 an hour they pay us is cheap compared to the deduction they can get."

Although Scott's company serves many YAP males who need "female judgment," women represent about 80 to 90% of the clientele: "Women intuitively understand that there is all this stuff in life that you might not get to."

Physical Fitness Consultant

Financial Consultant

Wardrobe Consultant

Female YAP

Male YAP

Decorating Consultant

Sample network of personal consultants

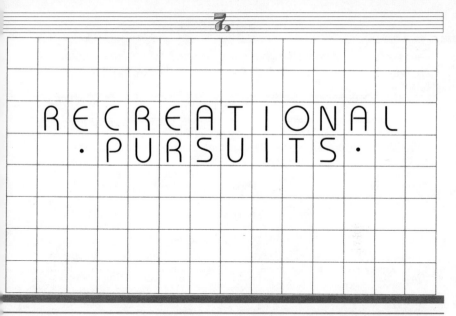

RECREATIONAL ·PURSUITS·

Gratifying Ways to Dispose of Your Income

Your hectic worklife creates a lot of stress. One of the best ways to alleviate excess anxiety is through meaningful recreation. Never just "hang around" during your leisure time—to others, this is a sure sign that your personal life is on the slow track. Besides, you need small talk for the office. Co-workers won't be impressed if you go home each night to read *People* magazine or watch *Family Feud*.

When planning leisure activities, YAPs take the following into account:

Firm Goals. Whether you begin an activity to lose weight, tone your muscles, or enrich your mind, announce your motive at the very outset. You do not perform a recreational task just for the hell of it. "Because it's there" might be a good enough excuse for mountain climbers, but it doesn't cut it for the serious YAP recreationalist.

Good Networking Possibilities. More deals are made on the golf course and racquetball court than in any other setting. Before choosing an after-work endeavor, be sure to check it out for possible contacts. A word of advice: avoid quilting, birdwatching, or any other pastimes in which most of the participants are housewives and little old ladies.

Huge Outlays of Money for Related Equipment. Inexpensive interests are no fun! To dispose of your income properly, choose cutting-edge hobbies that require large expenditures. For example:

High-Tech Pastimes

Inexpensive Hobby	YAP version
Reading the papers	Computer terminal hooked up to UPI wire service
Swimming	Scuba diving
Stamp collecting	Collecting netsuke, rare coins, or American Impressionists
Gardening	Indoor hydroponic horticulture
Playing Atari video games	Computer "hacking" with two IBM personal computers and a modem to interface with information services.

Other Non-YAP hobbies: Bowling, Sunday drives, walking in the park, body surfing (unless you are renting a beachfront house for $2,000 a month).

At home, a YAP relaxes with his 19th century billiard table
(the only type of pool table that's acceptable).

Exercising Your Options

Ideally, there is no such thing as a fat YAP. No true YAP will admit to extra poundage, because clothing manufacturers have yet to produce a good dress-for-success suit for *either* male or female chubbettes. But since you sit in an office all day, you'll have to work hard to keep your body as trim as your mind.

Fortunately, we have entered an era that glorifies exercise in all its forms, most especially when it is rigidly programmatic. Thus, after working "in," you can work "out." Choose among several approaches to stave off the effects of aging and excessive amounts of Oreo ice cream.

•*The Ersatz-ercises*: Especially popular with female YAPs, these exercise plans camouflage the agony of sit-ups, jumping jacks, and other excruciating bodily contortions with "fun" names such as *dancercise*, *jazzercise*, and *aerobics*. Before you sign up, check the musical accompaniment. Early Motown and the Stones are best, but sometimes you can get stuck with bad tapes of the Carpenters.

•*The Fully-Automated Resistance Torture Rack*: Nautilus machines are the best example of this exercise option. An instructor straps you into something left over from the Inquisition, and you're on your way to harder, larger muscles at only 20 minutes per workout. A favorite with all types of YAPs because of the time-efficiency factor, but especially appealing to gay male YAPs who favor the sculpted-body look.

•*The Yoga-Yogurt Trip*: Relaxing stretches and poses tone up your body and tone down your anxieties. Hatha yoga is the favorite, but T'ai Chi, karate, and judo are also popular. Artsy YAPs go in for this approach; Late-Bloomers and Bohemians sometimes teach some form of Eastern exercise. (It helps their bad backs.)

The Passive Solo Plan. Passive exercise doesn't take off pounds, but makes you feel better. You can either let weird machines do it for you, or indulge in personal massages that are supposed to get your body's energy channels flowing. Swedish massage, shiatsu massage, and Rolfing are favorite YAP mind and body stretchers.

Old sports and exercise techniques that are still in with YAPs: tennis, squash, jogging (with Sony Walkman), racquetball.

Y.A.P. Tip

The hottest new trend is personal fitness consultants, who for $25 to $100 an hour come to your home to bother you with aerobics, weight-lifting, and other exercise regimens. One personal trainer recently told a Los Angeles Times reporter: "Instead of going to a psychiatrist, clients work out three times a week. I wouldn't say they all enjoy it, but they know it's necessary."

Queen of the YAP exercise mavens: Jane Fonda (who else?) *Waiting in the wings:* Raquel Welch and Christie Brinkley.

  Non-YAP exercise stars: Richard Simmons, Jack La Lanne, Marie Osmond.

The Entertainment Scene

Like all other aspects of their lives, YAPs take their entertainment very seriously. Culture plays a major role in your selection of recreational activities. You should get something meaningful out of everything you view, be it a concert, movie, play, or even (and this gets to be more of a challenge) a television program.

If at all possible, purchase subscription ticket series to the local orchestra, ballet, and theater companies. Remember to pencil in these engagements in your datebook so that you won't make any other commitments for evenings allotted to cultural intake. (Also, devise a contingency plan for giving away the tickets you can't use because you're working late.)

Movies (known as "films") should be imported from another country if at all possible. (Australian cinema is the most acceptable English-speaking viewing experience.) Try to reside within taxi distance of at least one foreign film emporium, and *never* live in any city that doesn't show Truffaut films at least once or twice a year.

As for TV, a selected few commercial programs are permissible. But stick with PBS, and you'll never go wrong.

Favorite YAP *movie stars:* Joan Crawford, Bette Davis, Meryl Streep, Dustin Hoffman, Catherine

---

The Only TV Shows a YAP Will Admit to Watching When Not Gravely Ill

Hill Street Blues	Today
60 Minutes	MacNeil/Lehrer Report
Nightline	Masterpiece Theater
The CBS Evening News	Wall Street Week
Presidential addresses	Nova
Late Night with David Letterman	M*A*S*H (reruns)
Princess Di's Wedding (reruns of the	Cheers
original 6:00 A.M. live-by-satellite telecasts)	
Election coverage (state and national only)	
Sports (if your team is winning big)	

Defunct TV Shows YAPs Publicly Mourn

Dick Cavett	Taxi
The Paper Chase (but you can still catch it on cable)	Lou Grant

---

TV Shows that YAPs Secretly Tape on their VCRs

Dynasty	Leave it to Beaver reruns
Rockford Files reruns	Gilligan's Island reruns
Dukes of Hazzard	The People's Court
Dance Fever	General Hospital
Jerry Lewis movies	Donahue
The Tonight Show	Star Trek reruns

Deneuve, Woody Allen, Diane Keaton, William Hurt, John Heard, Faye Dunaway, Jill Clayburgh, Mariel Hemingway, Mel Gibson, Gerard Depardieu, Mary Tyler Moore, Jack Nicholson, Donald Sutherland, Katharine Hepburn, Jane Fonda, Ben Kingsley, Jessica Lange, Peter O'Toole.

Non-YAP movie stars: Burt Reynolds, Clint Eastwood, Charles Bronson, Valerie Perrine, Leslie Ann Warren, Barbra Streisand, Divine, Dolly Parton, Bruce Lee, Chuck Norris, Stella Stevens, Farrah Fawcett, Charlton Heston, Pia Zadora, Marilyn Chambers, Nick Nolte, Elizabeth Taylor.

All-time YAP film classics: Kramer vs. Kramer, An Unmarried Woman, Ordinary People, Betrayal, Apprenticeship of Duddy Kravitz, Return of the Secaucus Seven, Fantasia, Network, Annie Hall, Manhattan, My Dinner with André, Casablanca, King of Hearts, Harold and Maude, All About Eve.

YAP Radio Listening

Any classical or jazz station (preferably public radio).

Generic "easy listening" rock 'n' roll stations that play lots of Beatles, Motown, Simon and Garfunkel, Harry Chapin, Carole King, Bob Dylan: for those who are over 30 or who haven't bought a new record since 1975.

"All Things Considered" on Public Radio.

"Prairie Home Companion" with Garrison Keilor on Public Radio (Bohemian YAP).

Non-YAP: "Hot Hit" teenybopper AM stations, talk stations, Muzak easy-listening stations.

The Necessary VCR: Making TV Fit Your Schedule

Because you're a busy career person, your day doesn't end at 5 P.M. Why should you be forced to adapt to the prime-time schedules that networks and cable stations have decided upon for everyday, ordinary viewers? Invest in a video cassette recorder (VCR). Tape programs, and you'll never again need to endure late-night commercials for mattress companies. You can also buy and rent movies to show in the comfort of your own home.

The Shopping Experience

YAPs don't shop just anywhere for their take-out food, clothing, greeting cards, and *objêts d'art*. Specialized boutiques and quaint shopping centers abound with items carefully chosen to make you feel your disposable income is buying something truly unique. The typical YAP shopping district falls into one of four categories.

The Waterfront Development: Like lemmings, YAPs are attracted to the sea. And rivers. And lakes.

Any place that's near the water automatically takes on the aura of romance that you should demand from the Shopping Experience. Waterfront restaurants built on wharfs and piers feature spectacular views.

The Historically-Certified Building: Former firehouses, torpedo factories, canneries, stock exchanges, wire warehouses, and other utilitarian structures have been gutted and fitted with

The Historically-Certified Shopping Experience

atriums and skylights, spaces for tiny boutiques and eateries, and flagpoles for brightly-colored nylon banners. Names of the individual shops allude to the building's original use. Walls are emblazoned with enlarged vintage photographs of the building and the workers who inhabited it in "the old days."

The Slick Urban Mall: Located near the business district to attract the lunch crowd, this plate glass, textured-concrete structure was built on the site of a parking lot or an older, more elegant building torn down to make way for it. Fancy neon-sculpture logos adorn some of the stores; large weeping fig trees decorate passageways. Glass elevators add that special touch.

The Open-Air Market: Where working-class people used to get their vegetables, pasta, dead rabbits and live chickens. Now the home of outdoor boutiques and pseudo-ethnic food stands. Weary shoppers dine alfresco beneath colorful umbrellas.

In any YAP shopping area, you can find unique items in the following types of stores:

Sophisticated Greeting Cards. The most unique wrapping paper you've ever seen, printed in Europe or on recycled paper. Cards feature pop-up cutouts of '30s film stars and/or airbrush paintings of stark naked men. Owners care about the very best, but *never* carry Hallmark.

YAPs typically buy funky greeting cards to save the time of writing letters.

One-Theme "Cute." Entire shop is organized around products relating to one subject: bears, hearts, pigs, boxes, kites, or unicorns (usually the owner's Magnificent Obsession). Sample names: The Bear Necessities, Go Fly a Kite, Hog Wild.

Gourmet. Sometimes specializing in only one delectable goodie—cheese, natural foods, chocolate, popcorn, or cookies—and variations thereof; sometimes combining them.

Scandinavian Chic. White cotton sofas, white cotton rugs, corduroy loveseats that pull out to form foam beds; yellow, red, blue, and purple stackable cups; butcher-block and teak dining room tables, director's chairs, handblown wineglasses, stackable wire storage bins, wooden dish-drying racks, and other goodies inspired by the Lifestyle of the Midnight Sun.

The Nouvelle Baby/Toy Shoppe

Clothing Boutique. Specialties range from dress-for-success shops to way-out, funky leisurewear. Never do they sell underwear, corsets, or other mundane "foundation" garments.

Handmade Heaven. Hand-thrown stoneware, hand-stitched quilts, and hand-dipped candles from Vermont, Appalachia, or other areas with low wage scales.

Nouvelle Baby/Toy Shoppe. Oshkosh overalls in many fabrics, pint-sized LaCoste shirts, silk-screened jumpsuits, batik T-shirts, and leather purses for the toddler set. Also a good selection of durable, expensive natural-finish wooden toys and fiendishly imaginative stuffed animals, vegetables, and minerals.

Upscale Five and Dime. Magazines, paperback books, penny candy that costs 4¢ apiece, outrageously overpriced stickers for the back of envelopes; pens shaped like tools, vegetables, and other, more obscene objects; deliberately-tacky ashtrays, candles that resemble

The Upscale Five-and-Dime, where YAPs go to buy all their toys

desserts, tinted notepaper sold not by the box but by the pound, wind-up toys, and pencils with cleverly-designed erasers.

Shopping by Mail, or How You Can Learn to Love (800) Numbers

The booming business of direct-mail merchandising was tailor-made for the YAP existence. You can save lots of time by ordering necessities and gifts from the spate of glossy, full-color catalogs that arrive in your mailbox almost daily. Unless you have a helpful neighbor to pick up the package from your doorstep or apartment lobby, make sure to have companies send your order to the office. (If you *do* have a helpful neighbor who's actually home during the day, chances are you don't live in a YAP neighborhood. You should do some serious thinking about your property values.)

The Most Amazing YAP Mail-Order Product

Porcelain Häagen-Dazs cups and plates—exact replicas of the gourmet ice cream's paper packaging, from the *Epicure* catalog. Set of four, dishwasher-safe 6-oz. cups and 5½" plates, *only* $35! Imagine how amused your friends will be at your next dinner party.

A Selective List of YAP Mail-Order Catalogs

For *gadgets and housewares:*

Brookstone, 127 Vose Farm Road, Peterborough, NH 03458

Conran's, Mail Order Division, 145 Huguenot St., New Rochelle, NY 10801

Hammacher Schlemmer, 147 East 57th Street, New York, NY 10022

The Sharper Image, 406 Jackson St., San Francisco, CA 94111

For *dress-for-success togs:*

Brooks Brothers, 346 Madison Avenue, New York, NY 10017; 1500 Chestnut Street, Philadelphia, PA 19102

St. Laurie, 84 Fifth Ave., New York, NY 10011

Jos. A. Banks, Clothier, 109 Market Place, Baltimore, MD 21202

For *kitchenware*:

The Chef's Catalog, 3915 Commercial Avenue, Northbrook, IL 60062

Epicure (Batterie de Cuisine), 65 E. Southwater, Chicago, IL 60601

Williams-Sonoma, Mail Order Department, P.O. Box 7456, San Francisco, CA 94120

For *objects d' art*:

Smithsonian Catalog, 900 Jefferson Drive, Washington, DC 20560

The Ebury Collection, 115 Powdermill Rd., Maynard, MA 01754

Metropolitan Museum Catalog, 5th Avenue and 82nd Street, New York, NY

YAP Shopping Centers and Areas Across the Country

Atlanta:
Peachtree Plaza

Baltimore:
Harborplace

Boston:
Quincy Market, Faneuil Hall
Newbury St.

Cleveland:
The Flats

Minneapolis:
Butler Square

City Center
Saint Anthony Main

New York:
The Market at Citicorp
South Street Southport

Philadelphia:
The Bourse
NewMarket

Phoenix:
Fifth Avenue in Scottsdale
The Borgata

Portland, Oregon:
The Galleria
The Yamhill Market

San Francisco:
Embarcadero
Union St.

Toronto:
The Eaton Center

YAP Travel

Leisure-time travel can help you get rid of tensions along with surplus money. However busy you are at the office, try to get away at least once a year. (Vacation stories occupy the top rung on the scale of office small talk, and can keep co-workers attentive for weeks.) You should seek out exotic locales—after all, you've already traveled to America's major cities on business (if not, pretend you have). In planning trips to unusual vacation spots, credit cards come in very handy. You might want to apply for a few airline cards to expand your vacation horizons.

The increased number of "learn-

When on vacation, seek out country restaurants with chalkboard menus.

The Ultimate YAP Wishbook: The Sharper Image

If you ever feel overworked and under-appreciated, just open up *The Sharper Image* and you'll remember *why* you need all that extra money. This catalog speaks to the hopes, dreams, and anxieties of every YAP in America. President Richard Thalheimer, whose picture and hearty greeting adorn the order form, has packed its pages with more gadgets and glitter than any individual could possibly consume.

Trying to manage your stress? Choose from among Calmset, an electronic tension-monitoring device ($149), Antache Biofeedback Earphones ($129), and a palm-sized biofeedback monitor ($99). Interested in toning your body? Order the Ultimate Rowing Machine ($349) or the Deluxe Gym ($409). Worried about your weight? Buy a Diet Trac computer ($49.95) or Cal Count pocket calculator ($69), or one of the numerous digital scales the company offers. Paranoid about phone taps? Send for the Phone Guard ($49).

Learn about the "new science of speed listening," made possible by a tape recorder that electronically skips over blank spaces between words and syllables, letting you listen to information at double-speed without distortion for only $199. Choose from several phone-answering machines and countless cordless phone sets. Or if you're feeling aggressive, select the authentic (but nonworking) replica of the Thompson Submachine Gun ($175) or the "space age" Commando Crossbow ($399).

It's one catalog that definitely deserves a place on your coffee table. Can't wait for the catalog to arrive? Then call their toll-free number—(800) 227-4365. Or tune into the Sharper Image Living Catalog on Satellite Program Network (SPN) or Modern Satellite Network (MSN). (Female YAPs: 1983 marked the first edition of The Sharper Image *Women's* Catalog.)

YAP autos: Saab, Audi, BMW, Citroen, Peugeot, Volvo, VW Rabbit, Honda Prelude, MG, Mercedes, Datsun 280Z, Jaguar Sedan, DeLorean, touring cars of the '20s and '30s.

Non-YAP: Vega, Pinto, Toyota Corolla, Datsun 210, Cadillac, Oldsmobile, Ford Mustang, Lincoln Continental, Chevette, AMC Pacer, Jeep, VW "Thing," TransAm.

---

ing vacations" offered by resorts around the world is a real boon to the workaholic YAP. You can depart without guilt, knowing that you will return with yet another skill to list on your résumé. Travel to Paris—but enroll in Cordon Bleu's five-week advanced cooking course ($1,000). Or attend Marcella Hazan's School of Classic Italian Cooking for two weeks in early summer ($1,250). In Greece (a very "in" country for YAP travel), learn Cretan cuisine for a week ($1,485 including airfare and lodging). Overseas and domestic wine classes also make fine vacation excuses. Go to the wine school in New York City's Windows on the World, or to Napa and Sonoma counties in California, or to the German Wine Academy in a 12th century monastery near Frankfurt.

Other learning vacations let you study photography, skiing, tennis, golf, fly-fishing, and sailing. The very best is one arranged by Club Med and Atari. On Punta Cana, the Dominican Republic's east coast, guests can use any one of 52 computer terminals to learn BASIC (a computer language) and how to plan budgets and balance a checkbook on a personal computer. Club Med also has computer banks at Caravelle on Guadeloupe and at Eleuthera in the Bahamas.

"In" YAP Vacation Spots: Europe (especially Portugal, Greece, Yugoslavia, France and Spain); Africa, China, Thailand, parts of the Caribbean, the Napa Valley, New England, Alaska, islands almost anywhere (as long as they are underpopulated).

Non-YAP Vacation Attractions: Disney World, Miami Beach, Busch Gardens, Six Flags over any State, the Grand Canyon of Pennsylvania, the Jersey Shore, Hearst Castle, Knott's Berry Farms, Sea World, historic shrines, any place that affixes a bumper sticker to your fender before you return to the parking lot; any town or city that sells souvenir T-shirts, key rings, or salt-and-pepper shakers.

Serious Interfacing

YAP Romance, Marriage, and Remarriage

Ambitious people have healthy sex drives. Sooner or later, every YAP realizes that it's more fun to eat gourmet take-out food in another person's company than alone with Dan Rather. But even though you interface with many people in your daily office setting, you may find it difficult to locate exciting members of the opposite sex to date. Your busy schedule—and frequent business trips—can isolate you from the swinging singles' scene. Besides, since you're well-educated and involved in a stimulating career, you aren't about to fall for anyone who's less than extraordinary.

The bar scene is still a popular way to find romance (or at least meaningful sexual experiences). But no true YAP has the time or energy to be a Happy Hour habitué. An expensive professional dating service that screens its clients can provide you with successful, ambitious persons of the opposite sex—who will understand that their relationship with you must somehow take second place to your 80-hour work week.

To locate such a professional dating service, *do not*

- Call (800) numbers advertised on late-night TV.
- Consult backs of matchbooks.
- Answer ads for executive escorts.

Instead, check glossy, upscale

103

regional magazines (New York, Chicago, etc.) for advertisements couched in professional language. For example: The Direct Way, a professional research corporation in San Francisco, aims its advertising at YAPs. The headline reads "Romantic Relationships: ANNUAL REPORT." Or if you're a short YAP, an East Coast dating service promises to match "single professionals 5'4" and under." And a serious ad for a service called Connections promises the lonely YAP that "an in-depth interview with our staff psychologist allows us to know you and to come up with the right person."

If you're a technology freak or mild exhibitionist, try one of the many video dating services available. One small video agency says it specializes in "too's"—the "too smart, too busy, too selective single professional." Introlens, the nation's largest, has seven franchises in New York, New Jersey, and Pennsylvania, serving about 17,000 members. The agency advertises itself as "the progressive, classy, and dignified way of meeting people in the '80s." For a membership fee of about $40 a

"You will meet a tall, dark, handsome man and you will beat him out for a promotion at the office."

month, a client gets to star in a personal, videotaped sales pitch and view other YAPs' video presentations. Then the dating service matches tapes and invites both man and woman to scan each other's presentations. If both are interested in meeting, a date is arranged.

Video introduction services have their advantages. If the match works out, you'll be able to play back your very first meeting on the VCR for your grandchildren. But presenting yourself on tape also requires a certain *savoir faire* that not every highstrung professional can command. (In a

---

The Ultimate YAP Video Introduction

Discouraged because your video dating service isn't finding you the right people to date? Consider the plight of Santa Monica resident Mark Halberstadt. In 1982, he made a two-minute, $2,000 film called "What Do You Think of My Face?" that flashed his telephone number over his image in local movie theaters and on Home Box Office cable TV. Despite some two thousand calls from women, Halberstadt claims to have had fewer than 10 dates after placing the ad. "There are about 10 million single women between 20 and 35," he recently told the *Los Angeles Times*, "and of those, maybe only 100 would be ideal for me."

year or two, there will be personal video-dating presentation con-sultants to minimize your on-screen tics.)

How to Know You Are in a YAP Singles Bar

- The golden oak bar sports potted ferns.
- Bar munchies consist of Pepperidge Farm goldfish, popcorn with herbs, or cheese and crackers.
- People leave business cards in cracks in the bathroom walls.
- They serve vintage wines by the glass.
- The jukebox is playing *Rubber Soul*.
- The bar television shows *On Golden Pond*.
- The blender is constantly whirring, mixing up frozen straw-berry daiquiris.
- Men and women are wearing business suits at 9:00 P.M.
- Waitresses wear white oxford shirts and red ties.
- The bartender used to be a clinical psychologist.

C.E. networking at her local bar

For Women: The Name Game

A female YAP should *never* take her husband's surname upon mar-riage; nor should a YAP groom ex-pect her to. Keeping your own name will cause a lot of social con-fusion and some funny looks from hotel desk clerks, but the status is worth the aggravation—it reminds everyone around you that there are two professionals in the family.

Y.A.P.
tip

Hold your wedding in a public place that rents space for special occasions. You can always claim a charitable tax deduction.
Never invite your ex-husband or wife to your wedding, even if you "get along just fine."

A Hyphenation Guide

Examples of impressive hyphenated last names:	Unwieldy hyphenated last names:
Schaefer-Green	Kirschenbaum-Gillespie
Vaughn-Sterling	Crenshaw-Diarchangelo

(Plus you get the added pleasure of having people occasionally address him by *your* last name.) Worried that Aunt Emmie and Uncle Harry won't get the point? Print up obnoxious announcements trumpeting the name retention and enclose them with your invitations.

A YAP woman has the option of hyphenating her surname with her husband's, but this tells the world that you haven't really decided *what* your role is. (And, nine times out of ten, the YAP husband will not hyphenate his last name to match.) Hyphenation works best when one of the last names is short. Otherwise, your surname begins to sound like the name of a law firm or pharmaceutical company.

Ironically, though hyphenation is not the most radical name strategy, it makes a woman very visible as a feminist. "Oh—you're one of those hyphenated types," is a comment heard frequently by one YAP female we know.

The Personal Ad Route

Glossy magazines usually reserve whole sections for "personal ads" placed by people looking for fun (defined in *many* ways), romance, and sometimes marriage. Also check out publications devoted entirely to personal pleas for love, such as *Intro* on the West Coast. Answering personal ads is much less expensive than a professional dating service, but you are also on your own, with no consultant to separate the YAPs from the weirdos, car mechanics and ne'er-do-wells. Writing your own ad gives you a sense of control,

---

The Office as Dating Service

You spend much of your time at the office anyway, so why not fall in love there? Until recently, almost all companies discouraged involvement between workers. But according to *Savvy* magazine (the Bible of executive women), a new study suggests that office affairs increase the productivity of women by 15%, and men by 17%.

---

since *you* do the screening of "applications." Always request a photograph, and make the person leave several messages on your phone machine before getting back to him or her. (See "True YAP Confession," p. 85.)

To put your best foot forward, your ad should contain:

•A *strong intro phrase.* Avoid a stream of shorthand descriptive letters (DWJMSOS, etc.). Instead, opt for a gripping lead-in that will capture the reader. Tried-and-true approaches include listing your profession (Attorney, Physician, Executive) or a more emotional, sensitive phrase ("Romantic Dinner for Two . . ." "As Time Goes By . . .").

•*Language emphasizing your successful career.* Let's face it, people will scrutinize your ad for anything that seems to say "loser." It's not the time to be shy—lay it on thick. (To get ideas for yourself and your brilliant career, see p. 108).

For Female YAPs Only: Where Are All the Men?

In YAP women's conversations, a familiar theme is the dearth of single men. At any all-female gathering, you're likely to hear one or more of the following explanations of why it's hard to meet eligible men.

1. *The Pseudo-Historical Theory.* Proponents hold that the pool of single men was diminished by the Vietnam War, and that many of the young vagrants on the street would actually be eligible professional bachelors if not for the trauma and drug habits brought on by duty in Southeast Asia.

2. *The Married/Nerd Theory.* Simply put: All the good men are *already* married. If they're not, they're nerds.

3. *The Sociological/Demographic Theory.* Men tend to date bimbos younger and less educated than they are. YAP women do not often meet these under-qualifications.

4. *The Psychosexual Theory.* Educated, sensitive, interesting men abound—they're just attracted to men with the same qualities.

5. *The Jeanne Dixon–Martian Theory.* (You hear this one only in bars after 1:00 A.M.) Several years after soothsayer Jeanne Dixon accurately predicted President Kennedy's assassination, she prophesized that Martians would land and carry off all citizens under the age of 18. A few YAP women believe the Martians *did* land, but carried off only the male half of the minor population.

6. *The Tootsie Theory,* or *Cinema vérité.* Eligible men are everywhere, but in disguise. Any day now, a woman you admire tremendously will doff her wig, makeup, and falsies to reveal herself as the man of your dreams.

• A *devastatingly witty line*. Let your reader know just how clever you are. One YAP female we know was attracted to an ad that read: "Perhaps a lasting relationship? If not, we'll always have Paris."

• *Little or no mention of sex*. YAP ads cannot be lustful. Remember, you're writing only because you want someone with whom to share the finer things in life.

Key words and phrases to look for and use in personal ads to contact other YAPs: Professional, attractive, educated, bright, upwardly mobile, successful, secure, active, slim, serious, self-confident, energized, intelligent, executive, dynamic, power.

Red Flags (Avoid answering ads that use these words and phrases): Discreet, earthy, meaningful relationship, Amazon, sweet young thing, fine moral character, curvaceous, wealthy gentleman, benefactor, Cinderella, Prince Charming, lady who needs financial assistance, old-fashioned, TV [does *not* indicate an interest in video!].

The Least YAPpy Personal Ad We've Ever Seen

"Unprofessional, unsuccessful, unattractive, unintelligent, uninteresting male, 38, looking for female with similar qualities."

How to Share A Man: a YAP Dilemma

The *Wall Street Journal* reports that in Washington, D.C. (where the ratio of adult women to adult men is 6 to 5), two female therapists are holding a workshop, "Man-Sharing: Dilemma or Choice (And for Whom)," to help busy professional women "develop strategies for controlling their situations."

Want to get rich quick? Start a dating service for young professionals or, better yet, moneyed older people. Entrepreneur Neal Sheldon, 23, of Largo, Florida, has earned more than a million dollars since founding Execumatch, a dating service for millionaires. So far, he has matched only 30 wealthy clients with other rich people, but for his matchmaking skills, he charges clients $100,000.

For mature lovers established in their respective careers, Cupid's arrow is more like an acupuncture needle. You've been around a while, perhaps lived with a few people, and definitely gone out with many other successful professionals. You have felt the flush of romance, but you're not young or naïve enough to believe that getting married will change your whole life. In fact, chances are you've been married before. (See "Divorce," p.112).

When you marry, make sure to downplay the big event. Every aspect of a YAP nuptial should be *tasteful*, including the bride and groom's nonchalant attitude. A YAP bride-to-be *does not* run around talking about china patterns or showing off her engagement ring. Instead, she discusses strategies for fitting the wedding in around her business trip to Houston. A YAP bridegroom worries about last-minute details in his pre-nuptial financial agreement.

For a while, the "in" YAP wedding was an elopement to City

The tasteful YAP wedding cake (For the second or third marriage, omit one tier.)

Hall. The bride wore a business suit, feeling very sexy and much like Joan Crawford or Bette Davis in all those "career woman" films from the '40s. But YAPs are now getting married in a more tradi-

---

YAP Wedding Faux Pas: No-Nos for Serious Professional Weddings

Wedding cake with bride and groom on top (must always be tasteful flowers, preferably alstroemeria lilies).

Smashing cake in each other's faces.

Throwing the garter.

Announcing, "Ladies and gentlemen, for the first time, Mr. and Mrs. John Jones!"

Lots of bridesmaids.

Self-written ceremonies.

Dancing the hokey-pokey.

Getting drunk.

tional fashion. Although parents play a small role in planning the event, the couple usually plans all the *tasteful* parts of the ceremony and sometimes foots most of the bill. The bride wears a white linen or silk suit or, if she's under 32 and feeling romantic, a long white cotton dress from Laura Ashley. (For the groom, a black tuxedo, *sans* ruffled shirt, is perfect. But a nice new suit will do.)

Following your brief and tasteful ceremony (where all the guests may or may not be in attendance), a catered cocktail party or sit-down dinner is *de rigeur*. Plan a nouvelle, scaled-down feast. Consider adding at least one *unique*

feature to your wedding, such as a hot-air balloon or a classical string quartet. Unless you've both saved enough vacation for a three-week European museum hop, keep the honeymoon to a minimum. You don't want people at the office making special allowances just because you're getting married.

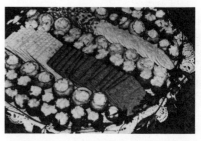

Prelude to a tasteful nuptial feast

Croissant sandwiches, perfect for the casual connubial feast

A YAP Wedding Checklist

Places for YAP weddings: Small chapels, renovated historical buildings, restaurants in old town houses, tents on parents' lawn, art galleries, City Hall (with tasteful party afterwards), public parks.

Non-YAP places for wedding receptions: VFW or Knights of Columbus halls, fire stations, school gymnasiums, catering halls, Holiday Inn conference rooms, basement rec rooms of suburban tract houses.

YAP wedding food: Paté, puff pastry, crudités with dip, exotic cheeses, interesting *hors d'oeuvres,* poached salmon, croissant sandwiches.

Non-YAP wedding food: Potato salad in the shape of a wedding bell, beef stroganoff, Jell-O with canned fruit, American cheese slices.

Music: classical or jazz (some Beatles, Billy Joel, and Motown acceptable).

Songs the band should never play at a YAP wedding: "Tie a Yellow Ribbon 'Round the Old Oak Tree," "Red Roses for a Blue Lady," "We've Only Just Begun," "Alleycat."

Acceptable selections for "your" song: Billy Joel's "I Love You Just the Way You Are," any old jazz tune ("Satin Doll," etc.) or Cole Porter song. (Caveat: At one YAP wedding we attended, the first tune the band struck up was "The Lady Is a Tramp." The marriage lasted 9 months.)

Unacceptable selection: "Having My Baby," "Close to You."

YAP honeymoon locales: Bed and Breakfast inns, areas with quaint wineries, a friend's (or your own) vacation home, a suite in an expensive hotel (only 1 to 3 nights) in a city where you will do business the following week.

Non-YAP honeymoon destinations: Niagara Falls, the Poconos, Bermuda, Epcot Center.

Extreme Types of YAP Marriages

The Commuter Marriage. Wife and husband work in different cities during the week and commute back and forth on weekends. They spend a lot on phone bills and Amtrak, but save on contraception costs.

The Bi-Coastal Marriage. A more serious version of the commuter marriage. Massive MCI bills and many bad in-flight movies to be endured. Couple has advantage, when the time comes, of comparing divorce laws and fees on both coasts before filing.

Can the Mixed Marriage Work? Can the marriage succeed if, say, a Bohemian YAP weds Mr. Junior Executive? Or a male SuperYAP marries a female Politically-Liberal type? Sometimes. In fact, as long as both partners display aspirations to get ahead in their fields, it's often better if they are not competing directly with each other in the same job market. Any marriage between a Hard-Edged Female YAP and Mr. Junior Executive, for example, would be fraught with complications.

YAPs can get into serious trouble if they wed unambitious types (Non-YAPs) who whine constantly about how the YAP spouse is never home. Avoid marrying people without careers, or anti-capitalist types (Marxists, socialists, anarchists) overtly hostile to YAP goals of money and success. *Excep-*

tion: Some less-sophisticated male YAPs still like to marry unambitious, undereducated females who enjoy performing menial household tasks, thus saving them the trouble and expense of hiring outside help.

True YAP Confessions

I Was a Slow-Track Wife

"My husband and I married in college. After graduation, I worked as a copywriter to support us while he studied for his M.B.A. After he got his degree, we went to Indianapolis, where he took his first job. Then he started playing the headhunter game and jumped at every offer he had, job-hopping from city to city. I moved with him each time, quitting my last job and starting a new one, sometimes at much lower pay.

"Over a candlelit dinner one evening—a week after I had started working my fifth low-paying job in three years—my husband announced that he was leaving me. When I asked why, he said, 'Because I've already got a fast-track career, and now I need a faster-track personal relationship.'

"I was stupefied at the time, but now I think I understand what he meant. The woman he left me for was younger, prettier, and—most importantly—more successful in her career. She had a glossier job title and a salary three times mine."

Divorce: The Obligatory Rite of Passage for the Serious YAP

Divorce is a YAP's badge of honor. Unless you've gone through at least one split, you're not taken seriously in many circles. Divorced YAPs look even more

112

committed to their careers than single or married YAPs, simply because their personal traumas didn't affect their work lives.

The two best kinds of YAP divorces are:

1. *Divorce from a slow-tracker.* You mistakenly thought this person had career plans of his or her own, but your graph is peaking while your spouse is plotting a horizontal baseline. After the separation, you can tell your friends that you and your ex-mate "didn't share the same goals."

2. *The Mutual-Agreement, Cordial Divorce.* Carried off by a surprising number of YAPs, this divorce is amiable and has the air of a dissolved business partnership. When you talk about your ex-spouse, friends could swear you're talking about a company you used to work for.

Divorces YAPs *do their best to avoid*: The Adulterous Divorce, and the proverbial "Messy" Divorce.

True**YAP**Confessions

We Ate Divorce Cake

"It was a second wedding for me. My husband and I had a wonderful reception in a greenhouse in a public park, catered by friends. One of the highlights was the three-tiered raspberry framboise wedding cake with peach-colored icing and flowers on top. The caterers saved the topmost tier for us to freeze and eat on our first anniversary.

"Several weeks past our anniversary, we'd both been working late for a while and had barely any food in the house. Then we remembered the cake in the freezer, and ate it for breakfast on a Tuesday morning. 'Hey,' said my husband as we drove into the city, 'do you realize that we just ate our wedding cake on the fifth anniversary of your divorce?'"

LAP-YAPS

A New Generation of Overachievers

"I have a brain and a womb, and I plan to use both."
—Congressperson Patricia Schroeder

Conceptualizing the Next Generation

Having concentrated on fast-track careers through their twenties, many YAPs finally begin to yearn for domesticity. "We never thought we'd want children, but . . ." sheepish couples confess. Yet once YAPs take to the idea, they embrace parenthood with the same fervor and commitment they brought to their careers. Demographers say that the United States is now experiencing an Echo Baby Boom. One gourmet take-out shop owner believes "there are two big status symbols now—food is one, and children are the other."

Because YAPs just don't have children casually like Mom and Dad did, female YAPs have deferred childbearing until their mid-thirties or later. But when they do start thinking about progeny, they

A BUSINESSMAN AND BUSINESSWOMAN AND THEIR BUSINESSKIDS

Prioritizing for Pregnancy: Are You Ready for Parenthood?

Use this checklist to see if a child will fit into your personal strategic plans.

☐ Are you over 30?

☐ Do you get misty-eyed when you see babies in the park?

☐ Do you call your spouse "Mom" or "Dad" in front of your cat, dog, or goldfish?

☐ Do you earn enough money to pay for full-time day care and the very best private nursery school?

☐ Would you think nothing of spending $300 for a pinstripe maternity business suit?

☐ Are you fairly sure your formal education is completed?

☐ Have you been to Europe at least three times?

☐ Have you ever spent more than 10 minutes in the presence of a two-year-old?

☐ Are you prepared to sell your white couch and put the Japanese porcelain collection in storage?

Score:

Between 5 and 8 "yes" answers: Proceed to the next step—strategic planning for conception and birth.

2 to 4 "yes" answers: Put pregnancy on the back burner for a while, or incorporate it into long-range strategic plans.

0 or 1 "yes" answers: Double-check your method of contraception.

---

quickly make up for lost time. They read *everything* on the subject of child-rearing, and are prepared when it comes time to decide.

Bringing children into the world is an important job. You should give the subject plenty of strategic thought so that your future offspring get every advantage they'll need to succeed in a fast-track world.

The five rules of YAP parenthood:

1. *Every child is a planned child.* Some couples time conception so that birth occurs conveniently during a two-week summer vacation. Not everyone can be so precise, but remember that for YAP couples,

there is no such thing as an unplanned pregnancy. If yours was an accident, lie.

2. *Money is no object.* Part of planning a pregnancy is making sure that you are financially secure enough to buy all the necessary baby accessories (see below) and do without some income for a short time.

3. *"We" get pregnant.* Starting a family is a project that takes both partners' energies. Today's YAP husband knows as much about prenatal care as his wife does.

4. *Careers continue.* Pregnancy and childbirth represent minor blips on the career electrocardiogram. Within a few months (or weeks, for the SuperYAP couple), the baby is

in an infant center or at home with a full-time caretaker—and you're both back at work, doing better than ever.

5. *What you do* now *will impact on your baby's future life and career.* Real YAPs leave nothing to chance. Your baby's education during his first three years will determine his success. If he doesn't get into the right day-care center, you can kiss Harvard goodbye.

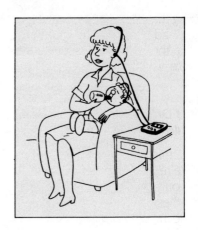

Labor Negotiations

It is not uncommon for couples to interview several obstetricians before deciding on the best medical advisor for their "pregnancy project." Husband and wife each take a long lunch hour and arrive at the ob/gyn's office armed with a list of questions. For YAPs, the only way to go is natural childbirth or the Lamaze method, because you want some control over your experience. You should also try to have your baby in a Birthing Center rather than a hospital. "It's beyond natural childbirth now," says one YAP father. "It has to do with taking responsibility for everything. It's okay now to decide the kinds of drugs you'll have during the pregnancy. In a way, you've become the doctor."

According to one gynecologist whose clients are professional women, many couples ask a written guarantee on the types of drugs the doctor will use during labor and other details of the delivery, down to circumcision. "I keep telling them that childbirth is a natural thing and I can't guarantee anything," says the baffled doctor.

A new YAP mother agrees: "People read so much about childbirth that when it comes time for them to actually go through it, they think they can call the shots like a business deal." People she knows ask prospective doctors questions such as "What would you do if I was in labor for more than 24 hours?" and then rate them on their answers. More often than not, YAP husbands want to be present at gynecological examinations, since the pregnancy is a joint experience.

Taking responsibility also involves bearing pain during labor and delivery. The overachiever's competitiveness emerges when YAP couples swap stories about childbirth. "They really rate you on how much pain you put up with," says one YAP father. "Women will brag that they didn't use anesthetics," adds his wife. "That implies that the other women who did were weak or just couldn't hack it."

The Dress-for-Success Maternity Wardrobe

It might be fashionable to say "we're pregnant," but let's face it—only one of you has to buy new clothes. Until recently, most available maternity outfits were pink and blue with little-girl smocking and bows at the collar—hardly businesslike attire. But now magazines like *Savvy* and *Working Woman* feature fashion layouts of well-designed (and expensive) clothing for the pregnant YAP.

The Mothers Work catalog (P.O. Box 40121, Philadelphia, PA 19106) caters exclusively to the expectant executive, offering conservative maternity business suits and blazers. "The image that your clothing projects is especially important now that you're pregnant," advises the catalog in its "Problems and Issues" section. "Unfortunately, a pregnant woman reminds many people of hearth and home rather than the boardroom."

Single Pregnancies: A New YAP Trend

Some career women, weary of waiting for Mr. Right to come along, are embarking on solo pregnancy projects. Having a baby outside of marriage is

An executive mother-to-be

nothing new: teenagers have been doing it quite well for years now. But older single YAPs have elevated the last-ditch-effort pregnancy to a status activity.

Strategies for conception include artificial insemination, sleeping with a friend, and sleeping with a stranger. Some career women advertise for volunteer fathers, stating the terms of their agreement.

Herewith, an actual example:

BLUE-EYED BLONDE, excellent career, good home, quality background, wants to be impregnated by decent, healthy, intelligent male carrying Grade-A genes. No responsibilities of fatherhood, no visitation rights, and no further contact once I'm *enceinte*. Because this request comes from the heart, screwballs, perverts, and otherwise vapid young men will not be acknowledged.

Naming Your Issue

Your extraordinary baby deserves an extraordinary name—something unique, catchy or important-sounding that'll look good on a business card someday. Here are three categories you might want to consider:

1.*Cute-sounding Ethnic Names*. Like cuisine from other countries, foreign names appeal to the YAP's cosmopolitan self-image. Of late, Gaelic and French names have been particularly popular. But remember: a child's name should sound nice and not be *too* weird.

●*Ethnic Lap-YAP names*: Brigitte, Caitlin, Danielle, Erin, Fiona, Nicole, Tara; Brendan, Liam, Sean, Seamus.

●*Ethnic names seldom considered by YAPs*: Giuseppe, Alfonso, Vladimir, Boleslaw, Gunter, Dmitri, Bruno, Fatima, Pedro, Isadore, Moische.

2. *Old Testament Names*. Names from the first part of the Bible are very trendy, often sounding folksy and important at the same time. Make sure you know the story about your child's namesake so you can sound scholarly when people ask.

●*Biblical Lap-YAP names*: Abigail, Naomi, Rachel, Rebecca, Sarah; Aaron, Adam, Benjamin, Jeremy, Jesse, Joshua, Nathaniel, Noah, Seth, Zachary.

●*Biblical Names Seldom Used by YAPs*: Onan, Cain, Moses, Nebuchadnezzar, Jesus, Judas, Job, Lot, Solomon, Herod, Abednego, Shadrack, Meshak.

3.*Recycled Surnames*. Using surnames as first names has always been popular in the South and among the very rich. (It's said to be a good way to flatter the other side of the family, thus securing inheritances.) Now professional couples everywhere are delving into family surnames to come up with unique first names for offspring. Sometimes the YAP mommy's maiden name is used. Again, the trick is to find something that sounds different but not bizarre, and one that, when combined with a surname, won't make your kid sound like a Southern Gothic novelist.

Suitable Recycled Surnames: Read, Hunter, Anderson, Kelly, Sinclair, Carson, Hollingsworth, Rollins, Hanley, Miller, Thatcher, Clement.

Unsuitable Surname-names for Lap-YAPs: Zblikewycz, Quattelbaum, Dworkin, Eckenrode, Cockburn, Lipschitz, Fuchs.

Other popular (but *unique*) names for Lap-YAPs:

Boys: Austin, Brandon, Brian, Christopher, Graham, Jason, Jonathan, Justin, Kevin, Matthew, Nicholas, Trevor, Timothy.

Girls: Alexandra, Alison, Amanda, Amy, Ashley, Brittany, Emily, Heather, Hillary, Jamie, Jennifer, ·Jessica, Joellen, Julie, Kate, Kimberly, Kristin, Melissa, Molly, Sabrina, Shannon.

Non-YAP names: Kathy, Elmer, Mildred, Betty, Clyde, Dwayne, Donald, Debbie, Ethel, Edith, Nancy, Mary, Joan, Florence, Susan, John, Maynard, Norman, Thomas, Robert, Rodney, Fred, Bill, Bud, Butch.

Some Essentials for Bringing up Baby

Snugli Infant Carrier (corduroy or seersucker, *not* the cheaper, machine-made denim Snugli 2)

Perego or Aprica stroller (preferably with eight wheels)

Sterling silver comb and brush sets

Designer bib

Hand-made crib quilt

Christening or Bris outfit costing at least $75

Izod or Pierre Cardin jogging suit

Petit Bateau cotton underwear

Absorba cotton terry diaper set

Izod polo shirt

At Lap-YAP stores, even the socks spell success.

YAP togs: at $155, a leather bomber jacket is a must for the chic male Lap-YAP

Issue Management: Activities to Expand Baby's Intellect and Coordination

•*Gymnastics.* A generation that grew up with the President's Physical Fitness program could hardly be expected to let their tykes lie around getting flabby. In special programs such as Gymboree on the West Coast, parents help babies three months and older learn gymnastics and simple exercises.

•*Suzuki violin.* Nurture your budding Mozart with a miniature instrument he can play when he's two. (Another smart investment: earplugs.)

•*Infant Swimming.* In "Water Baby" programs, you can make sure your child is "drown-proof" before the age of six months.

•*Educational Programs.* Through the miracle of flash-card learning taught at places such as the Better Baby Institute (Chestnut Hill, PA),

Ambiguity of good and evil in Melville's moral cosmology.

INFARCT OF PULMONARY ARTERY.

your seven-month-old can learn to do simple arithmetic. Your eleven-month-old can read (even though he can't speak to tell you about it). Mom and Dad can also teach baby to identify Shakespearean characters and read Japanese and French. At the Small Bytes Computer School (Tucson, AZ), toddlers can learn to program.

Lap-YAPs discussing their day-care interviews

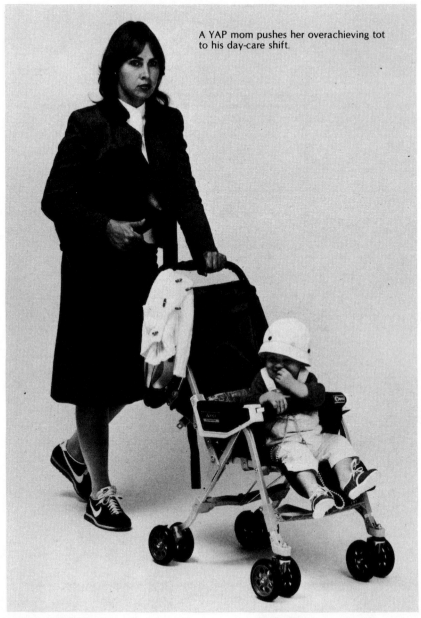

A YAP mom pushes her overachieving tot to his day-care shift.

Tips for Helping Your Kid Get Ahead

1. *Before s/he is born, sign up for day care and other educational services.* The wait for a good day-care center (especially one with a French name) and other important activities can sometimes be upwards of six

Non-YAP mother wasting precious opportunities for enriching her baby's mind

months. You don't want your three-month-old hanging around the house when all the other kids on the block are at Gymboree.

2. As soon as s/he can talk (or even a bit before), begin drills in interview techniques. Only well-prepared kids breeze through the nursery school admis-

sions process. When the interviewer asks, "How do you see yourself in five years?" your child should *not* answer, "In third grade."

3. *Always dress your kid well.* The baby dress-for-success suit (Izod shirt, Oshkosh jeans, Nike sneakers, and Shetland sweater or bomber jacket) shows that your child is part of a professional family. *Never* let synthetic fibers touch baby's body. *Never* buy anything at Sears or K-Mart.

Langdon, do a commercial for Mr. Cook.

A YAP child catching some CRT rays at computer camp

True **YAP** Confessions

My Baby Had Flash-Card Burnout

"When my son was about six months old, I started him on those 'better baby' flash card programs. For a little while each day, I showed him pictures of birds and flowers and trees. Then I started doing simple math with him. He seemed to be progressing well, and he would amuse Daddy by identifying flora and fauna flash cards.

"But once my baby began to talk in complete sentences, he seemed to get more and more hostile in our flash-card sessions. It got to the point where he would give the same answer for each card, even though he **knew** he was wrong. He's four now and doesn't seem to have the attention span of other kids his age. Sometimes I feel guilty that I ruined him at an early age."

About the author. . .

After a happy childhood in New Jersey, C.E. Crimmins taught macramé and hung around with potters until 1976, when she made the mistake of going to graduate school in English. After struggling for years to write a dissertation on Good Friday sermons of the 14th century, she left academia to write seed catalogs. Finally discovering her YAP identity, she joined a big-city consulting firm, where she learned the facts of fast-track life.

We would like to thank the following establishments for allowing us to take photographs:
Bloomingdale's (The Court at King of Prussia, PA)
Barry Leonard, Crimper (Philadelphia, PA)
Born Yesterday (Philadelphia, PA)
J.E. Caldwell Co. (The Court at King of Prussia, PA)
The Bourse (Philadelphia, PA)
Church English Shoes Limited (The Court at King of Prussia, PA)
Collander Data Products (Philadelphia, PA)
Conran's (King of Prussia, PA)
The Commissary (Philadelphia, PA)
Day by Day Restaurant (Philadelphia, PA)
Frog Restaurant (Philadelphia, PA)
Gargoyles Ltd. (Philadelphia, PA)
Karl's Juvenile Furniture (Philadelphia, PA)
Operatic Symphonic Barber Shop (Philadelphia, PA)
Philadelphia Running Center (Philadelphia, PA)
Philadelphia Trunk Co. (The Court at King of Prussia, PA)
Swan Galleries (Philadelphia, PA): Raku with Japanese Calligraphy by Jonathan Pressler; Round Vessel by David Bigelow; Geometric Weaving by Cornelia Breitenbach
Urban Outfitters (Philadelphia, PA)
H.A. Winston Co. (Philadelphia, PA)

The following stores and individuals were kind enough to provide photographs and advertisements:
Epicure (Batterie de Cuisine, Chicago, IL)
Mothers Work (Philadelphia, PA)
St. Laurie Ltd. (New York, NY)
The Sharper Image (San Francisco, CA)
The Support System (Philadelphia, PA)
Victor M. Votsch (Food Courtesy of E.A.T.S., Philadelphia, PA)
Victoria's Secret (San Francisco, CA)
Sharon Wohlmuth

And many thanks to our YAP models: Sarah Babaian, Debbie Barbee, Martin Bodtmann, Deborah E. Boyle, Joellen Brown, Barrington J. Brooks, J. Richard Conklin, Melissa Cookman, Douglas Cooper-smith, Christopher Curchin, Barbara Eberlein, Ella Straw Edwards, James Fanto, Alan Forman, Andrew Fruzzetti, Kathy Kiernan, Michael J. Koob, Deborah McColloch, Greg O'Brien, MaryAnn Osler-Teacher, Amy R. Podolsky, Brennan Preine, Dominick J. Santangini, Madge Schultz, Ellen Silver, Mary Straney, Lawrence Teacher, Matthew Teacher, Rachael Teacher, Stuart Teacher, Ronald Turner, Peter Read Urban, and Sharon Wohlmuth.